How to Work

By Amos R. Wells

Author of "How to Study,"

"How to Work," etc.

First Fruits Press
Wilmore, Kentucky
c2015

How to work, by Amos R. Wells.

First Fruits Press, ©2015
Previously published: Boston and Chicago: United Society of Christian Endeavor, ©1900.

ISBN: 9781621714255 (print), 9781621714262 (digital)

Digital version at http://place.asburyseminary.edu/christianendeavorbooks/11/

Wells, Amos R. (Amos Russel), 1862-1933.
How to work / by Amos R. Wells.
152 pages ; 21 cm.
Wilmore, Ky. : First Fruits Press, ©2015.
Reprint. Previously published: Boston : United Society of Christian Endeavor, ©1900.
ISBN: 9781621714255 (pbk.)
1. Success. 2. Christian life. 3. Psychology, Religious. I. Title.
BJ1611 .W4 2015

Cover design by Jonathan Ramsay

asburyseminary.edu
800.2ASBURY
204 North Lexington Avenue
Wilmore, Kentucky 40390

First Fruits
THE ACADEMIC OPEN PRESS OF ASBURY SEMINARY

First Fruits Press
The Academic Open Press of Asbury Theological Seminary
204 N. Lexington Ave., Wilmore, KY 40390
859-858-2236
first.fruits@asburyseminary.edu
asbury.to/firstfruits

How to Work

The "How" Series

By Amos R. Wells

How to Play
How to Work
How to Study

How to Work

By AMOS R. WELLS

Author of " How to Play," " How to Study," etc.

United Society of Christian Endeavor

Boston and Chicago

CONTENTS

HOW TO WORK.

CHAPTER I.

PROCRASTINATING AND PUTTERING.

WISH to give you my decalogue of work, my ten commandments of labor. And I want to write them, not on tables of stone, but on the fleshly tablets of your hearts. Now you each have two hearts, luckily, a right and a left one, joined together; so that I can divide my commandments into two tables, easy for you to remember. You are to fix the first table by the letter p. The commandments are: Do not procrastinate. Do not putter. Take your own pace. Read work's parables. Remember the promises. You are to fix the second table by the vowels, a, e, i, o, u. That is: Be ambitious. Be easy. Be intelligent. Be orderly. Be upright. That is the outline of what I want to say to you in these opening chapters.

The first commandment of labor is, Do not procrastinate. There was once a Yankee farmer whose acres were covered with bowlders, and very much needed stone fences. "I'll build 'em," said the Yankee, "to-morrow or next day, I guess." But after many to-morrows and next days a good fairy took him in hand. Wherever he walked, she threw great bowlders before him. He lifted them out of the way. She sent immense stones in front of his plow. He got a crowbar, and rolled them into the next furrow. She piled them on his wheelbarrow. In surprise he threw them off. At last she sent him a dream, —a dream of a stone fence, broad, square, neat, and strong, and far-reaching about his farm. "This is the fence," she cried in his ears, "the fence you might have made with the strength you used in throwing stones out of your way."

Do you ever think of this, that it takes a certain amount of energy to reject tasks when they press upon you for the doing, that the worry over an unaccomplished duty is a burden it takes strength to bear? Do you realize that I am speaking not in rhetorical exaggeration, but in literal exactness, when I say that procrastination requires power, and often a power that, when summed up, would do the deed? Oh, how we cheat ourselves! How we hammer away on cold iron! How we set the mill to grinding after the water has passed, so that we must laboriously turn the mill-wheel ourselves!

The waste of strength is not the worst of it. "By the street of 'By and By' one arrives at the house of 'Never.'" That's the worst of it. Putting off means leaving off. Going to do is going undone, ten cases out of nine.

Think of it. If the little grain of corn does not sprout in the springtime, the liberal summer and wide autumn and the whole round year has henceforth no abiding-place for it. But if it begins to grow in that acceptable time, the crowded summer will find space for the tallest stalk it can push up, and the full autumn can contain its heavy ears. This is the interpretation of the parable : there is no room in all the infinite future for a single deed that ought to be done now. So the first commandment of labor is, Do not procrastinate.

DO NOT PUTTER.

The second commandment about labor is, Do not putter. This is the second in the order of time, but the first of all in the order of importance. For a worker's prime virtue is vim. Yet there are thousands of workmen, so-called, whose practice, if not whose lips, read the text in this way: "Whatsoever thy hands find to do, dilly-dally with all thy might." "Puttery, puttery, puttery,"—that's what Tennyson's Yorkshire farmer would hear their horses' hoofs "sa-ay."

Apropos of horses, there is a fairy story about a horse, which you have never heard, and which you ought to know. It is this: Mary Ann was attempting to drive, one day, along a straight road; and before many minutes the horse knew what Mary Ann knew at the start, that she did not know how to drive. She held the reins loosely, then she pulled them tight. She jerked now one side and now the other. She flapped them. She got them crossed. She kept up a constant clicking with her tongue. She fussed with the whip. At last Dolly, the horse, who was a very sensible old horse, got tired of such nonsense, and called on the horse-fairies to interfere. (This is a fairy story, you know.) So straightway they came, and while one unharnessed Dolly, and changed her with a tap of a magic wand into a girl like Mary Ann, another changed Mary Ann into a horse like Dolly, and harnessed her in a jiffy. Then Dolly got into the carriage, and took her revenge on Mary Ann. And oh, such pullings and twitchings and flappings and jerkings! Mary Ann never forgot the lesson. Do you wonder what is the moral of my fairy story? It is this: Drive your business, or your business will drive you. Go at your work in a straightforward, sensible way. Hold firm reins. Don't jerk and twitch and flap and fuss. Don't putter. For if you do, then in stern reality, and no longer in ridiculous fable, the retributive fairies of worry and vexation and disappointment and impatience and wasted time and strength and reputation will harness your soul to the tasks you should have ridden upon, and you will be driven unmercifully by the very powers you were made to drive.

There is a beautiful word, which every one who aspires to the high title of "worker" must manage in some way to get into the vocabulary of his life. That word is "alert." What a picture flashes into our minds when we say it! "Alert,"—bright eyes, quickly moving as the Greeks loved to see them; body in nice equipoise ready for prompt obedience; motions delicate, exact, and swift; speech clear-cut, quiet, and steady. That word "alert" is the poetical form of our American adjective, "business-like," the opposite of "puttering."

A straight line, your geometries tell you, is the shortest path between two points. The same definition fits the word "alert," the word "business-like." It means taking the shortest and easiest way to your goal. Is it mastery of a newspaper? You may putter over it an hour, or by alert skimming along headlines and coarse type you may get the very marrow out of that newspaper in ten minutes. Is it writing an essay? You may putter over pen and paper for days, or, by alert watching of your mind and your reading, prompt jotting down of ideas, energetic blocking out of the essay, you may do it much better in one-fourth the time. Lazy folks, puttering folks, take the most pains, while they think they are taking the least.

The King's business requireth haste. And this is one good reason why Christ's yoke is easy, because He teaches us to carry it with business-like alertness. There is a best way to do everything. That is also Christ's way, the easiest and shortest. The night cometh, when no man can work. Do not procrastinate. Do not putter.

CHAPTER II.

O not procrastinate. Do not putter. We must set alongside of these the third commandment of labor: Take your own pace. Any good driver could tell you what would happen if you should harness up short-pacing Dolly with long-pacing Dobbin. The necessary compromise would wofully tire them both.

You remember Dr. Holmes's felicitous comparison of the short-legged man to the little Dutch clock, briskly ticking his way through life, while his long-legged brother is the eight-day wall-clock, with its solemn and slow vibrations. Well, people's minds are just that way. And the little fellow may have the eight-day mind, and the tall fellow the brisk little Dutch-clock mind, and it would beat Time himself if you should force them to vibrate together.

Let me take a stride of two feet, nine and one-half inches, and I can walk twenty miles without stopping; but force me to keep step

13

with a stride of two feet, eight and one-half inches, or with one of two feet, ten and one-half inches, and I should be worn out in eight miles. This is one of the first truths that a teacher is made to learn, in that school where he is receiving lessons as fast as he gives them ; and I do not believe that the great Teacher of us all is less considerate, or that he expects as much from his dull scholars as from his bright ones.

This is the one danger in reading inspiring biographies. They are likely to urge us to the futile imitation of men and women whose pace is longer and swifter far than ours. And when we try that pace, as some will, we are apt to draw no other conclusion from our cer- tain failure than that their way is not our way. It might be our way, if we took our pace to it. These great men and women may be able to learn twenty languages, master a dozen arts, write poetry and novels and ser- mons, and play ten musical instruments, do- ing it all well, and you think you can do it.

You have been fooled by this that fools us all, at one time or another. Everybody carries about with him the germs of power to do al- most everything, and sometimes he finds this out,—finds out that he has music in him, and poetry, and art, and skill to do nice handiwork, and strength for the hammer and the plough, and a tongue to move men. And then he begins to develop them all, and gets into the same scrape I did this summer.

I thought it would be nice to have my own flowers, that I might not be obliged to depend on the floral charity of my neighbors. So I spaded up a bed about four feet by two, made nice little trenches, filled them with seed, covered them up, and waited in faith. I put into that little bed one paper of phlox, one of mignonette, one of sweet alyssum, one of asters, one of dahlias, one of zinnias, and, for good measure, one of something I did not know. All my seeds sprouted finely, and you may fancy the result. I am glad I had that experience, because the present condition of that flower-bed furnishes the best illustration on this planet of the sage phrase, " Jack-of-all trades, master of none."

" The question is not," says Souvestre, unwisely, " to discover what will suit us, but for what we are suited." That is not the question at all. Too many things are possible for us. The question is to discover what of all our possibilities God wants us to develop. Paul might have been a distinguished orator, statesman, philosopher, general, author, merchant ; but he said, " This one thing I do."

Power and inclination call in many ways; duty, only in one. Take that one way and the pace in it that God has made natural for you, neither fretted because others get along faster than you, nor proud because you are permitted to surpass others; and you will be crowned with Paul's crown at the end of the way. Do not procrastinate. Do not putter. Take your own pace.

CHAPTER III.

THE fourth labor commandment is, Read work's parables. Did you ever notice that just two-thirds of Christ's parables are based on events in some business or other? Shepherds, bankers, merchants, housewives, farmers, fishers, stewards, lawyers, day-laborers,—all find their occupations illuminated in these marvellous stories. How much Christ must have thought of human labor!

But did He exhaust the parables of work in those twenty-nine short stories? They were given for examples merely, to teach us how to regard these occupations of ours. We are to make our work a college and a church; and broom, saw, plough, and yardstick are to teach us and to preach to us. George Herbert, after all, has written the true psalm of labor :

> "Teach me, my God and King,
> In all things Thee to see,
> And what I do in anything
> To do it as for Thee.

  •   •   •   •   •

"All may of Thee partake ;
   Nothing can be so mean
Which with this tincture, 'For **Thy sake,**'
   Will not grow bright and **clean.**

"A servant with this clause
   Makes drudgery divine ;
Who sweeps a room as for Thy laws
   Makes that and the action fine.

"This is the famous stone
   That turneth all to gold,
For that which God doth touch and own
   Cannot for less be told."

With one line only of that priceless poem I am inclined to quarrel. No one can "make drudgery divine," for it is already so. But, alas! how many poor drudges do not discover the divinity of their drudgery, do not touch it with that "famous stone" of consecration which "turneth all to gold," do not read the parables of labor as Christ read them!

Let the clerk in a drug store see that he may be an assistant of the great Physician. Let the farmer's boy know that the seed, even the literal seed he plants, is a word of God. Let the young mechanic see in saw and hammer reminders of the world's Carpenter. Let the cook bethink herself that her bread may be bread of the higher life as well as of the lower, and that the flesh she prepares, if the

Master's spirit be in the preparation, may be meat indeed. Let the busy housemaid, as she sweeps and garnishes, prepare that house for the seven spirits of blessedness. Let the earnest student of surveying, philosophy, zoölogy, never forget that all ways lead to the one Way, all truths to the one Truth, all life to the one Life. These are some of work's parables.

O that I could emblazon this thought on the soul of every worker in the world—that the secret of all joy in labor is in these words, "my Father's business"! My teaching, your studying, farming, housework,—our Father's business. That thought once fixed in the world's commerce, greed would die, dishonesty would hide its head, hearts weary of trifles would exult in them, hearts anxious for results would grow grandly confident, for would not God care for His own?

Except the Lord built the house, they labor in vain that build it. . . . It is in vain for you that ye rise up early, and so late take rest, and eat the bread of toil. For the Lord giveth unto His beloved *in their sleep*,—not in their sloth, but in that restful dependence on Him that prevents anxious lying awake, since they have read the parables of their work and know that they are about their Father's business.

A few decades hence, at best, and how
clearly each of us will know this! How, in
the revealing light of that day, what we call
our real practical work will fade to the thin-
ness of a fable, and that higher parabolic
meaning which lies hidden in our work will
stand forth as the one real and practical thing
of all, to crown us or condemn us!

Do not procrastinate. Do not putter. Take
your own pace. Read work's parables and
ponder them.

The last commandment on the first table is

REMEMBER THE PROMISES.

There is a tool that every carpenter must put
into his tool-chest, or the fullest chest is empty.
There is an ink into which every author must
first dip his pen, or the blackest ink will be invisible. There is a word that every student
must read before he can understand a line of
his text-books. That tool, that ink, that word,
is faith. The universe is full of promises.
Better be "a blind spinner in the sun" of
these promises than own sharpest eyes which
cannot see them.

What are these promises for the worker?
One is history, which is a crowded procession
of toilers rewarded,—some soon, some late,
but all gloriously. One is nature, whose every

rainbow promises seed for the sower and bread for the eater, whose liberal fields, rich sun, and fruitful seasons are crammed with guaranties for labor from the Father who worketh hitherto. One is our own spirit, which in its loftiest moments sees that everything is good and just and no toil unrewarded. One is God's written Word, a long promise of joy to those who labor together with Him.

I watch the noble young men as they try to open the doors of this world. Some apply a gold key; that is genius. Some have keys of flashing silver; they rely on zeal. Iron keys are borne by others: they are the plodders. And for all these the bolts fly back, to be sure, but the doors remain obstinately closed. But I see a few who carry, in addition to their keys of gold or silver or iron, a tiny key that glitters like a diamond. This they thrust into an unnoticed cranny of the heavy doors, which fly back eagerly to give them entrance. Those diamond keys mean confidence—confidence in God, trust in the order of things, faith in one's self and one's fellows.

" Can he work?" " Has he brains?" " Has he tact?" These are not the first questions that the world asks about a young man, but, strange to say, it is this: " Does he expect to succeed?" If the answer to this is " No," or

a half-hearted " Yes," all is up with the young
man; but if he believes in his life, the world
believes in him. The cynical old maxim is an
untrue one: " Nothing succeeds like success."
Let the young workman adopt a bolder and
more genuine principle: " Nothing succeeds
like the expectation of success." Learn that
your rightful endeavors are in the line of a
literally resistless current of promises. You
have half learned how to work when you have
learned that. Remember the promises.

CHAPTER IV.

E have filled out the first table of commandments about labor, which we were to remember by the letter P: do not procrastinate; do not putter; take your own pace; read work's parables; remember the promises. Now I must treat my second table of commandments with undeserved brevity. These five were to be fixed by the vowels, A, E, I, O, U.

First, be ambitious. A great man once wished to select from a crowd of applicants a teacher for his young boys. "Now for a test," he said, "you shall each show me how you would teach my sons to do one of the simplest things, to break a stone in two." So he led them to a pile of bowlders. The first took the hammer, and quite dexterously split a slab of limestone. "Very neat," remarked the great man, "but limestone is easily broken." The second, with a shrewd blow, parted a mass of hard quartz. "Better," said the great man; "but something is lacking still." The third

23

chose one equally large piece of quartz, broke it nicely, and then selected a very tough bowlder of greenstone. The hammer fell sharply, and the obstinate stone was shattered. "That's what I want my sons taught," said the great man,—" to go on from what is hard to what is harder."

The great man understood what parts mediocrity from success. The first is content with mastery of the difficult. The second takes to heart Browning's grand words:

> "Ah, but a man's reach should exceed his grasp,
> Or what's heaven for?"

"Good things are hard." That was Plato's favorite saying. But Plato himself would agree that what is good fades to worse and worst unless the worker goes on to harder and hardest. Be ambitious.

Then, be easy. That is, never be contented until your work has become second nature to you. You know how the young girl learns to play on the piano. How like witchery it seems, as her white fingers flash rippling along the keys, moving them to obedient music! But that pliant dexterity came by way of stiff knuckles, aching muscles, weary hours, strong patience, and the " try " that means "triumph."

Do you remember how it was when you

learned to ride the bicycle; how tensely you
held your arms, and how bent was your mind
on turning your wheel to balance the push on
the opposite pedal; how your brain whirled
and your shoulders complained at the end of
your first mile? Now you pedal instinctively,
and you turn the wheel to and fro with no
consciousness of effort.

And the girl does not really play the piano,
nor the boy ride the bicycle, nor any worker
do any work at his best, until this thing has
happened to him, that his work has become his
play. "What we must do," says Coleridge,
"let us love to do." It is a noble chemistry
that turns necessity into pleasure. And so
against our sixth labor commandment, Be ambitious,—go on from hard to harder,—we must
hasten to set this seventh, Be easy,—continue
at the hard work until it has become play to
you.

Next, be intelligent. Add to your work
that last important item in the old lady's rec-
ipe for bread. "Stir in a little judgment,"
said the dear old soul. You want me to esti-
mate the yield of that wheat-field? Let me
see. Rich, deep loam. Good situation.
Ought to give twenty bushels to the acre. But
stay. Let me see the farmer. That stupid,
lazy lout? The field will not give ten bushels

to the acre. I am wrong, and the farmer is that thoughtful young fellow, crumbling the soil in his hand and examining it with such care? His field will give thirty bushels to the acre, such a good year as this. "As the man is worth, his land is worth," says the shrewd Frenchman.

"Stir in judgment." Do not make two trips of it with one hand full when the filling of both hands might finish it in one trip. Do not run upstairs to bring something down and then go up again to take something up. Do not go down town for a stick of sealing-wax, and after your return bethink yourself of the meat you must get for dinner. Do not hunt through the book page by page, when a glance at the index would show you what you wish.

The old proverb is right. "Contrivance is better than hard work," not merely because it is more economical of God-given strength and time, but because it puts our work on a higher plane. For what does Ruskin tell us? "It is only by labor that thought can be made healthy, and only by thought that labor can be made happy." Be intelligent, then, as well as ambitious and easy.

CHAPTER V.

"O, U" WORKERS.

B E not only ambitious, easy, and intelligent, but be orderly, too. I wonder how many thousand lives have been straightened out by that fine admonition from " the old English parsonage down by the sea," " Do ye nexte thynge." It has unwound the tangle of my life many a time, and when duties pulled this way and that, when time was short and work was long, and a maze of worriment surrounded me worse than any Cretan labyrinth, this was a better clew than Ariadne's to lead me into clear ways again,—" Do ye nexte thynge."

There are some men whose idea of order is like this, that at 7 A. M. they will consume two eggs, a plate of hash, and a cup of coffee. At 7:30 they will put on a dressing-gown buttoned at the third buttonhole from the top. At 7:40 they will dip a stub pen into violet ink and write five and one-half pages of their new novel. And if anything is wrong with hash, buttonhole, or violet ink, all is over for the day, and they must wait until the next 7 A. M. for an orderly start.

The order of a worker who means business is not the order of a whimsical schedule, but the order of proximity. Take up your work vigorously as it presents itself to you. Get up a mental turnstile that will make your crowd of duties step forward one by one. Permit no jostling. Give yourself closely to the first as the experienced ticket agent does at the station, finish it, call out " Next," and let the turnstile turn the first out and another in.

My word for it, there's a magic in such a method that will seem fairly miraculous to a man who is in the habit of worrying about one task with one-half his brain, and planning another with the other half, while his hands are executing the third. Be ambitious in your work, easy, intelligent, orderly.

Finally, be upright. That is, be straight. Be honest. Give worth for wages. Despise from your very soul all braggart short-cuts to knowledge, to money, to influence and position. Work your way up. That's your only insurance against tumbling down.

These are golden words of Emerson's : " I hate the shallow Americanism which hopes to get rich by credit, to get knowledge by raps on midnight tables, skill without study, mastery without apprenticeship, power through a packed jury or caucus, or wealth by fraud. They think they have got it, but they have got something else,—a crime, which calls for another crime, and another devil behind that; these are steps to suicide, infamy, and the harming of mankind. In this life of show, puffing, advertisement, and the manufacture of public opinion, all excellence is lost sight of in the hunger for sudden performance and un-earned praise."

Let that never be said of you. I will not add more, lest you charge me with preaching. Cry " Excelsior," though your path lies all in the valley. Allow no endeavor to stop short of thorough performance. Be upright.

Now my second table is complete, bearing the exhortations to ambition, ease, intelligence, order, and uprightness in work. I must add one thing more; it is the gold, which, pressed into all the words thus inscribed on your heart-tablets, will make them shine with heaven's own light. That gold is prayer. Need I say to Christians that without that element all ten of these qualifications of the noble workman go for naught? Need I re-mind you of our height's littleness, of our sight's blindness, of our strength's utter feeble-ness before our commonest tasks? But there

is a Workman in our midst taller than the sons
of men, whose eye knows no barrier and whose
power knows no obstacle, and, best of all,
whose love speeds to our whispered prayers.
Are we workers together with Him ?

CHAPTER VI.

HOW TO FEEL LIKE IT.

HOW much easier we can work " when we feel like it " than when we do not! The task that on other less fortunate days hitches and halts and grinds like a bicycle with dirt in its bearings, now rolls itself off as smoothly and delightfully as a bicycle newly cleaned and oiled rolls off the miles. So true is this, that in many a piece of work quite half of the undertaking may be considered accomplished before you begin, if you only "feel like" beginning.

Therefore it is a very important problem for the practical worker, "How can I feel like it all the time? How can I abolish blue Mondays? How can I get rid of the sense of monotony? How can I keep my work always fresh, always interesting and enjoyable?" Such a spirit would be worth more to most merchants than a capital of a hundred thousand dollars, and some of them are sensible enough to know it and to plan their lives so wisely that they are always eager for their work, and go to it at the end of twenty years with the appetite and zest of a novice.

One of the secrets of the matter is that at the very start they took up work that they *could* like, work for which they were fitted, work in which they might reasonably expect to succeed. O, those poor girls that by the thousand are at this very moment pushing rebellious fingers up and down the ivory keyboard, with not a scrap of music in their souls, just because their ambitious mammas want to make pianists of them, though they are "dying" to crochet, or trim bonnets! O, those thousands of poor boys who at this moment are poring over law books that to them are dry as last century's leaves, just because their ambitious papas want to make barristers of them, while their own unfettered fancy would mount a horse and herd cattle on the great plains, or board a train to get particulars of the railroad wreck for the *Herald!* Can Susie be expected to like it? Can Tom be expected to like it?

But, granted that the work is a task that he is able to like, one way always to "feel like it" is never to wait till he feels like it, but to pitch into the work as soon as the time for work comes, with no reference to the feelings whatever. Lead forth the nag, though your head

aches. Jump into the saddle, though rheuma-
tism rebels. Canter away, with your teeth
clinched and your brows set. It will not be
long before your lips will begin to smile, and
the wrinkles will come out of your forehead,
and on the home stretch your eyes will sparkle
and your cheeks will glow, and you will feel
like it very much indeed.

The second rule is, " Don't stop till you *do*
feel like it." This is very important. Napo-
leon had what we have come to call the prestige of success. He had won in so many battles that his foes keeled over almost at sight of
him, to save him the trouble of knocking them
down. Stick to every pursuit, every task, until it becomes enjoyable, and you will acquire
for yourself just such a prestige, so that whatever distasteful undertaking you may approach
will say to itself, " There comes a man who
never leaves a task till he has subdued it ut-
terly, body and spirit. I might as well make
myself agreeable to him at the start." And it
will.

I suppose this is all there is of it, though
various subordinate thoughts might be pressed
home, such as these : In approaching a disagreeable task, first take up all the easier and
more agreeable portions of it ; conquering them
will give you a feeling of strength, and you

will say to yourself, "There is so much out of the way, and without difficulty; certainly I can accomplish what is left." Trick yourself into a game, as by saying, "Now let me see how many sticks of wood I can saw in ten minutes, and then let me run a race with myself the second ten, and then try to beat *that* record, and so on." Keep before your mind the result, the reward: the eye on the goal shortens the mile. Fall in love with processes. If you are painting a barn, see how far you can make a brushful go, and without spilling a drop. If you are baking a pie, think up some unique pattern with which to ornament the crust. There is no task, not even digging a ditch, but has interest and even romance in it, if you dig in the right way.

CHAPTER VII.

"WHAT!" you say, "can any kind of faithfulness be a poor kind?" Yes, indeed. Listen.

A mistress of a large house once assigned her four housemaids each to a room, to clean it and put it in order before noon.

The first housemaid, Susan, said to herself as she set vigorously to work, "Now there's Betsey. She thinks she's so smart. I'll show mistress who is the best housemaid here. My room shall be cleaned perfectly, and set in order before that conceited Betsey is half through." But though Susan worked faithfully, Betsey's room was finished first, and looked much nicer than Susan's. As soon as Susan saw this she threw down her tools and worked no longer. Her faithfulness was founded on emulation, and the superiority of her fellow-worker ended it.

Kate, on the contrary, set herself doggedly to her task, saying, "I'll make this a job to

35

be proud of. I propose to do it perfectly."
She began in a little corner, and scrubbed and
scrubbed, always seeing something more that
needed doing in that corner, until noon came.
The corner was perfect, but the rest of the
room untouched. And so Kate's overfaithful-
ness concerning a part of her task made her
faithless in regard to the whole.

The third was Milly, who was a very ambitious girl. "If I clean this room well." she
planned, "mistress may take more notice of
me, and let me wait on the children, or even
on herself, and then I may get to be governess,
and then—who knows?—I may even set up
a ladies' seminary of my own!" So Milly
worked very faithfully, her head full of such
ambitious plans. Too full, however, for, quite
engrossed in these enticing thoughts, she let
fall a magnificent vase, and quite ruined it.
So she became faithless in little things, because
her faithfulness in them was only through
hope of greater things.

But Betsey, the fourth, loved her work and
her mistress, and carried common sense and
sprightliness to her tasks. She took no thought
about the success of others, except to praise it.
She judged of the thoroughness expected, by
the time given to the task. Her one ambition
was to do her best in the present. And so it

happened that her work was accomplished first, and best.

Faithfulness which springs from over-fondness for details, from emulation or from ambition, is often very hard to tell from the true faithfulness. But it is not true, and nothing is true faithfulness which does not spring from love of the work, and love of the Master.

CHAPTER VIII.

WORKING TO BREAK THE RECORD.

HAVE grown very tired of hearing people talk about breaking the record. In my boyhood days a horse was thought to do something handsome if he made his mile in 2:40, but such a horse is nowhere nowadays, the record has been so badly broken. Every steamship captain who crosses the Atlantic is unhappy if he cannot bring back with him as part of his cargo a smashed record. Every sheriff who runs for office, no matter how well qualified for the position he may be, or how much the people like him, or what a respectable majority they give him, feels half-defeated unless in the election he has broken somebody's record. Newspapers strain every nerve to break the record of day's sales; locomotive engineers endanger lives to break the record of rapid runs; popular preachers do sensational advertising in order to break the record of big congregations; nay, even nations are infected with the plague, and if France builds a big ship, Germany must straightway build one a few inches longer.

Now I sometimes wish that I could take these poor, old, broken records in my arms, could mend them up and comfort them. They were getting along well enough; the world was acquainted with them and satisfied with them until some ambitious upstart came along and broke them, in order to patch himself up a crown out of the fragments.

Understand me now, my readers. I am not such a ninny as to snarl at progress, simply because it upsets some of my old-fashioned notions; only, it must be progress worth the making. Did you ever think what a vast difference there is between making a record and breaking it? When Tennyson wrote the sweetest lyrics of the world's literature he did not break any one's record, spoil any one's fame. People still read Burns and Shelley, Moore and Horace, with as much enjoyment as if Tennyson had never written. Tennyson simply made a sweet and noble record of his own. When Lincoln gained the presidency of the United States he did not break any one's record. Who knows or cares what his majority was, or whether Illinois gave him an unusually large vote? Mr. Lincoln made a record for himself which needs no lustre from the broken records of other men. Have you ever observed which of the monthly magazines brag most loudly of their enormous subscription lists and make boldest claims of predominance over all others? Does the *Atlantic Monthly*, or the other three which stand with it at the head of our American culture? No. The *Atlantic Monthly* would not wish to pose in the eyes of its readers as a record-breaker, but as a record-maker, a creator and not a racer. Consequently when we think of it we do not think of figures,—so many hundred thousand a month, so many tons of paper,—but we think of men, of Longfellow, Hawthorne, Holmes, Emerson, Whittier, and Lowell.

In fine, that is the mischief of this mania for record-breaking,—we get to thinking more of statistics than of manliness, more of the relations of our work than of the work itself. When a man is to be chosen for office, we look around not for the wisest statesman and the noblest Christian, but for the politician who can roll up an unprecedented majority. In selecting a plan for a vessel, the steamship company does not pay half so much attention to the comfort and safety of her future passengers as to the lines and construction which may diminish time a few minutes and give the ship a temporary record-breaking fame.

In choosing his writers and the subjects they are to treat, the average magazine editor has no thought for the effect upon the national literature and the national morals, but considers only or chiefly the probable totals of the subscription-books.

Does any one pretend that, for instance, this ceaseless breaking of the record in horse-racing is all to improve the breed of horses? Are modern racing horses a whit more serviceable than the old two-forties; or were these, in fact, of more use than plain Dobbin who never carried a jockey on his back? Does the great *Panoramic Monthly Universe*, with its half-million of subscribers and its yard-long list of " eminent writers " and " popular features," elevate perceptibly our American literature and life? Oh, yes; record-breakers always make money. But let them not make also the audacious pretence that they are improving character.

My dear young man or woman, I warn you that if you care to make any worthy record for yourself you must refrain from all thought of breaking the record of some one else. A record-smasher's record is sure to be smashed in its turn, but independent, original, manly, and modest work stands firm for ages of ages.

CHAPTER IX.

THIS chapter has nothing to do with tobacco smoke. I suppose I may take it for granted that my readers have nothing to do with it, either, except when some foul-mouthed fellow puffs it into their faces, and they must hold their breath for a block.

I want to talk, rather, about those dense, black, carbon-laden masses of hot air that rush out of our chimneys and locomotives, and fall to the earth to fill our lungs and befoul our dwellings within and without, or else rise into the heavens to darken the sun and blacken the clouds. In many cities this smoke emission, from tugs, factories, furnaces, locomotives, dwellings, has become a serious menace to public health, as well as an immense public discomfort.

There is scarcely a large city in the world that is not anxiously studying the means of removing, or at least checking, this nuisance.

42

In some cases it must be done by the adoption of brightly burning, almost smokeless, fuel, such as coke or anthracite or gas. In other cases it must be done by the adoption of various devices that burn the carbon dust entirely up, before it escapes into the outer air. In one way or another it may be done, and everywhere, nowadays, cities are demanding a reform in this important particular, and are making compulsory the use of some contrivance for the consumption of smoke on the premises where it is made.

Now I have spoken of this with a purpose beyond the merely material aspect. There is a spiritual smoke emission, and there should be a spiritual smoke consumption. No man ever lived so perfectly that he did not allow some fragments of his life to float off, black and aimless, useless and hurtful. No man's work was ever an absolutely clear flame, all his energies utilized in it, concentrated upon it. There's a ragged edge to all our endeavors, a residuum of unappropriated material.

For instance, we are about some noble task, and are trying so hard to accomplish it that we do not regard at all the little, black, impatient words and fretful, preoccupied frowns that fly off from the periphery of our task. Or, we are lost in thoughtful planning, and by

our very thought we are rendered so thoughtless of our immediate duties that black flakes
of discomfort sprinkle everything about us,
and even darken the sun. Or, we spend every
energy upon a single duty, quite heedless of
other duties, until a long, black column of failure caps a very feeble flame.

These examples, which you can multiply
indefinitely, are sufficient to show that it is
just as necessary in the spiritual as in the
physical world to consume our smoke, to
guard against leaving on the outskirts of our
tasks any mischievous remnants that may
wholly counterbalance the good our tasks may
accomplish. But how may this spiritual
smoke be consumed? How may we get to
doing clean jobs, living completed lives?

Here also, as in the world of carbon, two
devices are possible. As the men of chimneys
conduct the smoke, after it is made, back to
the furnace, and make it pass again through
the fire until every grain of carbon is burned
up, so we may do. We may keep zealous
watch over ourselves in our work, lay stern
hands on all escaping bits of passion, fretfulness, thoughtlessness, overanxiousness, and use
part of the fiery zeal wherewith we work, to
burn it up, and purify ourselves from it. That
is one way.

But the other method goes to the root of the matter : use smokeless coal. There is a fuel, wherewith we may feed our lives, that does not produce this mischievous residuum of annoying side-results. It is a compound fuel, made up of the love of God and the love of man. This, burning in our lives, gives off no smoke, though the least admixture of love of self raises a dense cloud. If our lives burn with this smokeless fuel, we may direct them to whatever tasks we will, sure that our labors, seeking solely the happiness of others, will not be marred by their discomfort or discredited by their hurt. Use smokeless fuel.

CHAPTER X.

BATTING, AND DOING THINGS.

HE great American game! The game which cuts a bigger figure in our newspapers (and possibly with right) than the great European game of war! The democratic game, around which cluster high and low, rich and poor, equally enthusiastic, and equally uncomfortable in the broiling sun! The game which in the eyes of the small boy divides honors with the presidency! *Baseball!*

An old professor of mine, in his youthful days, was considered quite a crack player in his college nine, and once in a long while, on the village green of his native hamlet, he swings a bat still to the admiration of the village club,—or are they laughing in their sleeves at the old gentleman: who knows? It was at a business meeting of this village nine, held at the house where I chanced to be staying on my annual vacation, that he, happening to look in upon the boys, was forced to remain; and after the business was com-

46

pleted, and it was finally decided who should play first base and who should be left fielder and who should pitch, there were vociferous calls for " Brownlow ! Professor Brownlow !" and he was compelled to make the following little speech :

" Boys," said he, " I played ball before you were born, and I ought to be able to give you a few pointers. You get up a good game, boys (loud applause), but I have noticed one serious defect. You are weak in the battery (murmurs of surprise and disapproval). O, I know you think that's one of your strong points. I suppose the stag is very proud of the antler that hangs him.

" In the first place, every boy of you bats for show, and not for the game. You glory in ' home runs ' and ' three-baggers.' I know how the spectators applaud when they see the ball rising so beautifully, high in the air, far out into the field. But you lost that last game of yours through those sky-scrapers. The other fellows did some easy fielding, and caught your ' flies ' every time ; while their batsmen, on the other hand, sent you hot ' liners ' and ' ground-scrapers,' and you could do nothing with them. They didn't get half so much applause, but they got the game.

" When you are at the bat, fellows, and, for

that matter, everywhere in life, you must not ask yourself first, 'How can I make a big record for myself?' but 'How can I put in my work so that it will be best for all concerned?' See whether any one is on first base or not. If he is, don't crowd him. If a man is on third, bring him in. Make a sacrifice hit. Strike at the ball even if it isn't just where you want it. Score points for the nine, not for yourself.

"Then, I object to the position some of you take in batting,—just for all the world like the attitude assumed by conceited young folks when they go out into life. Some of you carry your bat away back over your shoulder, making it necessary to swing it so far that all accuracy of stroke is destroyed. Then how you stand, as if you were posing for your picture, and wanted the camera to get a front view of the big red C on your uniform! *Here's* the way to stand (and with his cane he illustrated, amid loud applause). You are all ready, you see, to throw your whole weight on your left foot, to meet the coming ball. Your bat is given enough swing for a good momentum, and not too much for accuracy. And you strike the ball down, and not danger-ously up, ready for the fielders. There's nothing fancy about this. It's like a man's wearing his plain business clothes on business days.

"No, boys, I don't want to take the glory and the show out of your ball-playing, or out of your lives. It's all right to be pleased with applause. Only, wouldn't you a little rather have the applause at the end of the game, and let the other fellows get it through the first innings, if they can? In life and in baseball, boys, those most honored in the long run are not the 'highflyers,' not the showy and splurgy men, but the judicious, self-sacrificing workers, who seek the common welfare, and let their own glory come in where it will." (Loud applause.)

CHAPTER XI.

HERE is always a fairy land of science. This fairy land is filled with the things we know so little about that we say "Pooh! pooh!" at them. When we find out about them, we say "We always thought so," and then the fairies go somewhere else.

One of these fairy lands just now is that sleepy country known as hypnotism. Hypnotism is artificial sleep. In this, just as in most kinds of natural sleep, some of the faculties remain awake, and especially are they awake to the bidding of the man who puts the patient to sleep.

Indeed, in hypnotism, the faculties that do remain awake are more wide-awake than usual. President G. Stanley Hall, in one of his lectures, illustrates this finely. Take a long gas pipe from which projects fifty lighted jets. Then turn out the lights one by one. The lights that remain burn all the more brightly, until the last jet glares with great brilliancy.

So in the case of a mesmerized man, all the physical and mental energies seem to flow through the single channel that remains open. If, at the will of the doctor, he sees, then he sees with unwonted intensity and with grotesque imagination. If he feels, he is conscious of pressure that does not exist. If he is bidden to hear, his ear catches strains inaudible to all others. His memory is intensified, so that he will hold in mind the most complicated orders, and even execute them after he has waked, and on a distant day. But all this is only at the bidding of the hypnotizer. If *he* presents a wisp of paper as a rose, straightway it has beauty and fragrance; but if you or I should present a perfect Jacqueminot, the patient would neither see it nor smell it.

And now, my workers, how many of you are hypnotized? You shake your vigorous heads, and declare them wide-awake and self-commanded. But are you sure?

I know scores of men who are spiritually and mentally hypnotized. That is, nearly all the holes in their pipe of life are choked up,— nearly all the natural avenues of activity,— and their energy must be exerted hysterically and disproportionately through the few outlets that remain open. *Every one-sided man is hypnotized.*

Here's a man asleep on the physical side. He has no love for nature, no zest for bodily sport, for hearty food, for vigorous living. Here's a poor fellow asleep on the spiritual side. He knows no Sabbath, owns no closet of prayer, fears the dark, and finds it dull to be alone. Here's a man mentally hypnotized. He is interested in nothing but beetles, or Greek roots, or compound fractions. Here's a man socially hypnotized. He can see no good in artisans, or he has no use for rich folks, or he dislikes Germans, or he has an aversion for men who wear stovepipe hats.

Every hobby carries its rider swiftly into the dull land of hypnotism. And it's the easiest thing in the world to mount a hobby,—much easier than for the present writer to mount a horse. At first the hobby is a toy horse, and slips between your feet, you scarcely know how. But the hobby grows apace. Now he's the size of a goat. Now he's a donkey, and your feet are just off the ground. Soon he's a full-grown horse, and your feet are in the stirrups. Speedily he's a camel, and you are perched on the loftiest hump. And before you know it he's an elephant, and you are afraid to get down, if you want to.

Or, to go back to our first symbol. No man who is one-sided will confess it, any more than the mesmeric patient is conscious of his hypnotic condition. Indeed, among my acquaintances some of the folks who are most certain that they are unabridged encyclopædias are those whose minds do not even cover one letter of the alphabet. You see, they *are* using all their energies, and they are unconscious that they are pouring them all out of the same hole.

And finally, these spiritually and mentally hypnotized folks are not their own masters, any more than mesmeric patients are. Somebody or something hypnotized them at the start. Possibly it was a fascinating teacher, to whose "specialty" they gave themselves up, body and soul. Possibly it was a book, to whose ideas they became such stupid and absolute converts that no other ideas were thenceforth admitted to their heads. Possibly it was a taste, a fancy, a whim, indulged in blindly until it became supreme. Whatever it was, the poor fellow is no longer his own, but thinks and feels, hears and sees, at the mere suggestion of this teacher, or book, or taste, or habit of life, all the time believing, mind you, that he is his own master, and scorning the insinuation that his mind and soul are another's.

O, you poor, deluded, hypnotized, sick folks!

As the doctor slaps his hands smartly before the face of the entranced patient, so I would wake you up with a sharp exhortation: Be men! Be women! Do your own thinking! Use all your powers! Live all over! Light all the jets!

CHAPTER XII.

HE successful people are those who can take a hint.

There is a very ancient proverb that some people think a quotation from the Bible, which runs, A word to the wise is sufficient.

The successful people everywhere are those wise folk to whom a word is sufficient.

A word is all we'll get, anyway, to help us toward success. The world is full of hints to the hearing ear, the seeing eye, but it has no time to preach full sermons. A word here, a gesture there, is all it has for us, and if we would learn its lessons we must be apt at taking hints.

In the world of business how often this truth is illustrated! Here is a man whose stock is always stale, whose methods are always antiquated, whose prices are a week behind the market quotations, whose advertisements are stereotyped, who never used a telephone, whose tools were patented before the war, who takes none of his trade papers, whose house is mortgaged, brow wrinkled, heart discouraged and discontented.

And at his side, his shop in the same block, his farm joining fences, is the business man who has been wise enough to discern the signs of the times, who has had eyes to see and ears to hear the hints the world was giving him, whose stock is of the freshest, whose methods are of the newest, prices the current prices, advertisements piquant and novel, tools of the most improved pattern, who keeps the telephone hot, and devours the papers and books pertaining to his business. You all know that the last will succeed and the first will fail. And the last has had no one to lay down a course for him to follow, a system for him to pursue. He has succeeded merely because he has been able to take a hint from all sources.

In social life here are two young people, equally good looking, minds equally brilliant, character equally founded on the right, yet one will have hosts of friends, be followed everywhere by smiles of loving approval, and the other will be a solitary, not so much disliked as ignored. Nine times out of ten it's because one can take a hint and the other cannot. One is sensitive to see in a shrug, a frown, the expression of the eye or the tone of voice, the disapproval of those around him, and shrewd at remedying whatever in himself merited their disapproval. The other is blind and deaf even to the most plainly expressed criticism. One is quick to perceive by expression or attitude when others are ill at ease, and ready to put them at ease. The other has no eyes for others' constraint. One is a veritable spiritual thermometer, and knows instinctively whether his friends are sad or happy, hopeful or despondent, and adapts himself to their needs. The other is blind to the little indications of the unhappiness and discontent and joy and longings of his companions, and is joyful in their sorrow, and unsympathetic in their joy, and stolid in their times of aspiration, because he cannot read the parable of their faces. And the first will have many friends, and the second will go through life alone.

How conspicuous are the examples of this principle in the world of study and of science! Bits of wood had been pushed by eastward breezes across the mysterious Atlantic for centuries before the man was born who could take the hint and discover a continent. A little girl, the daughter of a Dutch spectacle-maker, was playing with her father's lenses.

Holding two out before her she cried suddenly, "O, father! how near the steeple is!" That may have happened many times before, but Hans Lippersey was a wise man, and that word was enough for him. The telescope was made, to do for astronomy what Columbus did for geography. To enumerate all examples would be almost to detail the history of science, for, from the fall of Sir Isaac Newton's apple to the day when that puffing teakettle sang of the steam-engine, and down to the present decades, when an all but imperceptible retarding of an almost invisible point of light is made to add a new planet to the system, and when a minute shifting of a line of light is forced to disclose to us the rate and direction of motion of the star which the light left years ago, all the triumphs of the human mind have been won by its power to read parables, to take hints.

And now may I not, must I not apply all this to the life of the Spirit, to the pursuit of things highest and noblest for the soul? Here, too, success comes to the man who can take hints; who has eyes for the sunlight and the sky; who can interpret the parable of the seasons; who can hear with intelligent ears the birds' morning hymns; who finds tongues in trees, books in the running brooks, sermons in

stones; to whom the sight of the meanest
flower that grows is sufficient for uplifting toward the flower's Creator. Success here comes
to the man who is open to the contagion of
faith, open to the contagion of cheer, open to
the contagion of love; to the man who is able
to live in others' lives, be strengthened by
glimpses of their belief, gladdened by a smile
out of their happiness, comforted and assured
by a single look which speaks of their love.
Success in the spiritual life comes to the man
who can take hints from the past, from history, from biography, from written words;
the man to whom a saying of Christ's is life-
food more than brain-food; to whom a deed
of a wise and great man is more than a fact,
—is an inspiration; whose reading is done
with his heart in his eyes. And most of all,
success in the higher life comes to the man
who can hear God's Spirit speaking to him,
whose conscience is prompt and sure to condemn and approve what needs blame and
praise, whose will is yielded to God's slightest
hints of warning or of guidance.

Busy men of old heard in the midst of their
toils two words, spoken in that clear voice
which can never die out of this world, two
words, " Follow Me." And the two words
were sufficient,—for the hearers were wise,—

and led them into an immortality of useful-
ness and honor and joy supreme.

So, from commonplace events, from the
everyday marvels of the natural world, from
books, from friends, from the Spirit within
and above, come promptings daily and hourly,
" Follow Me," to manhood and womanhood
and God. We who have ears to hear, let us
hear.

CHAPTER XIII.

HURRY UP!

EW virtues of the worker are more needed nowadays than serenity.

When a long-legged, raw recruit, with a stride like a pair of compasses, comes on the parade-ground, it is the drill sergeant's first care to tame the nonconformist's pace to ordinary measure. This he does by bidding the novice to walk for two hours on an elevated horizontal ladder, whose rounds are the due distance apart, and whose height from the ground insures careful attention to the matter in hand—under foot, I should say. Graduated from this precarious school, the soldier feels on the safe earth intangible rounds everywhere; and his step has become attuned to the regimental average. Even so—for here comes the inevitable simile —even so, I fancy, we are set to walking in these measured spaces of time, that we may learn how to bear ourselves in the portionless reaches of eternity.

Cautiously and sedately must our recruit

pace the ladder. It is his apprenticeship to the slow-marching dignity of his company. He could not run for office on that ladder. It is not the fall of stocks that excites a panic in his breast. "Corners," "deals," "combines," and other speedy ways of "getting there," are meaningless to him. Nor would he answer pleasantly if told to "hurry up." It is plod, plod, plod, and the reward, adoption into the resistless, glorious swing of the regiment.

As I said, possibly our whole life is a ladder-drill in leisure. If so, it is a query whether those who scorn that discipline here below will ever get time, in all eternity, to become accustomed to no-time. Manifestly, our space-devouring recruit would not look so ridiculous, spoiling the harmonious movement of his company, as a man to whom the present day means more than a thousand years to come would look, if set in a host who have learned to hold a millennium as a day. One heavenly spirit bidding another " hurry up ! "—the idea seems half impious. Yet the earthly existence of some very excellent people is summed up in those two words.

" Hurry *up,*" when all hurry tends downward ! "Time and tide wait for no man," so hurry up, ye heirs of eternity ! Hurry up with your marriage, and down into a leis-

urely repentance! Hurry up with an educa-
tion, and down into mediocrity! Hurry up
with your book, and down to oblivion!

Probably every one knows about the wonderful old fable that tells how Hercules, set-
ting out on the journey of life, was met at the
first fork in the road by two beautiful women,
Vice and Virtue, each of whom strove to per-
suade him to go with her. But the fable does
not tell how, when Hercules had chosen Virtue, like the sensible old hero that he was, the
twain came in their travels to a second fork in
the road, and were accosted by two very handsome men. One, who wore a flashing business suit and had a very jaunty air, advanced
promptly and said, " I am To-day. If you
would be successful in life, come with me, and
hurry up!"

The other, whose dress Hercules did not
note, so simple was it, but whose eyes were ex-
ceedingly beautiful and penetrating, said
quietly, "I am called Forever. If you would
have abiding success, come with me."

Said To-day with a sneer: " Pay no attention to him; he is a visionary. The present
moment is the only time you dare call your
own. Live with me, with To-day!"

Then Forever answered, " The present
moment is always dying, but the future is

never dead. I can teach you how to make the present alive with the life of the future."

"That fellow, with his far-off gaze," said To-day scornfully, "will make you miss every opportunity for immediate profit. Who are the millionaires, the merchant princes, the Napoleons of finance? They are men of the times, who live in the day, who grasp their chances speedily."

"Ah, yes," replied Forever with equal scorn, "and the gold they heap up is no more enduring than coined butter. Is there by the side of the dark river any bank that will give them a bill of exchange on heaven?"

To-day shuddered as he answered, "That's the way with Forever. He's always gloomy and talking about death. Come with me, Hercules, if you want a pleasant, happy life. Come, hurry up. Don't stop to think so like a dolt."

Then Forever laughed as he replied, "There will come a time, To-day, when your very name will be changed to Death, and your companions will shrink from you; but my name never changes, and though my comrades think me stern and hard at first, before long they count it all happiness to live with me."

To-day interrupted impatiently: "This Forever, Hercules, is one of the most impracticable creatures imaginable. He would have you take a course in the fine arts, to improve your mind. I would send you to some man of business, and set you to work at once. He would have you study history before entering politics, but I would have you join yourself immediately to a man who knows how to get votes."

Then Forever interrupted in his turn: "You are strong, Hercules. Remember how you became strong. Was it not by making every day serve the future? Was it not by enduring immediate pain and hardship, and by eating only the plainest food, always looking not to the muscle and vigor and pleasure of the day, but to what you expected as the result of the day's privations? And was not that the most practical way of becoming strong, dear Hercules?"

Hereupon To-day set up a tremendous clamor. "Time flies, Hercules! Make hay while the sun shines! Every moment you delay here is worth a dollar! The present calls you, to make money, to win applause, to gain power. Be bold and business-like. The world is his who hustles. Come, hurry up!"

But by this time Hercules had made up his mind, and clasping hands with Forever, said, "I will go with you, dear master. For I think you will give me all that To-day offers, and very much more."

And so it happened that through all these centuries the world has never forgotten Hercules and the glorious life he lived.

And now let me lay aside ladder-simile and Hercules allegory. The world is made up of two sets of people—those that live for the fleeting moment, and so must be ever in a hurry ; and those that live in the moment for all eternity, and so live unfretted lives.

Once I went to see an exhibition of Gustave Doré's pictures. As a boy, I had been fascinated with the spirited work of this artist as I saw it represented in engravings, and I anticipated a rich treat in seeing the glorious originals. But, alas! though a few of them met my anticipations and were brilliant indeed, most of them were only immense sheets of dull colors, some of them mere ghosts of pictures peering out of a world of black. Doré did not use properly made colors, and so his paintings scarcely outlasted the life of the artist himself.

It is said to be thus with the much admired work of the great Hungarian painter, Munkacsy, who painted " Christ before Pilate " and " Christ on Calvary." He was very fond of the use of bitumen, which imparts exceeding richness to pictures, but must be used with great caution or it will turn the painting black. But Munkacsy used it lavishly, and some of his most valued works are already almost indistinguishable. Of course the knowledge of this peculiarity has operated to diminish greatly the prices paid for his paintings.

But Doré and Munkacsy and other careless artists are not the only ones that use perishing pigments. Many an ambitious youth is doing the same with his life. He would be rich in a hurry. He has no time to complete his schooling. He plunges into trade from the grammar school or the high school, rises for a while, and then, when it is too late, finds himself rapidly passed in the race by the wiser boys that took time to make ready. Or, he would shine as a scholar, but scorns the years of toil necessary to make himself master of what has already been wrought in his chosen field. He puts out a piece of flash writing or crude speculation, that wins a temporary success, but is speedily forgotten, having merely served to stamp him as a hopeless mediocre.

Or, there is the rich man who has so devoted himself to money-getting that he has lost the power of enjoying his wealth after he gets it. There is the young married man, who, after winning the object of his choice, finds himself too busy to take satisfaction in his home.

There is Martha, so fuming over household tasks, needlessly magnified, that she has no time for her Saviour. There is the young pianist, who has practised so ardently as to lame his hand for life, and the young teacher, who has studied so hard without exercise as to break down in the first good position. Yes, the world is full of these lives that are painted with bitumen.

O *festina lente*, make haste slowly. There is no surer way to waste time than to hurry too fast. Certainly the Creator knows how to get things done, and with what superb serenity and masterly leisure He proceeds about all His tasks! His paintings endure, every one of them. His pigments never fade. And as we become His apprentices, and dip our brushes into His patience and His peace, marvellous colors will begin to glow on the canvas of our lives, colors that not all the sunlight of time will obliterate.

I often see the expressive word, " Rush !" hastily scrawled on commissions of all kinds. Now it is written on a drawing sent to an engraver's, and the finished engraving, that a few years ago would have been the proud work of a week or a month, must be in the art editor's hands the next day. Sometimes these imperative four letters are written on a proof-sheet that accompanies a page of type sent to the foundry, and then they mean that even electricity must put its best foot foremost, and complete the electrotype within half a day. Sometimes the order for an edition of a book is thus emphasized, and then it means that a volume which not many decades ago an entire printing establishment would have required months to turn out, must ·be in the hands of the readers within a week.

It sometimes seems to me that I can read this word everywhere, " Rush! Rush! Rush!" on the electric cars, instead of the street signs; on office doors, instead of the familiar " Push " and " Pull "; on the faces of the hurrying crowds that scramble along our sidewalks; on the front of railway stations; nay, that I can even hear the word now and then in the bells of certain churches! Could a more appropriate word be found to emblazon on this century's escutcheon?

Now, most of this is wrong. Of course emergencies will arise when the utmost speed is necessary, but they are not half so frequent as we think they are; and at least half of the emergencies that at the time are necessities would not have been so, had proper forethought been exercised.

But we do not *plan* for restful lives, lives

that move without jar or friction. We have got into our heads the insane notion that a man, to be "smart," must always be in a rush, and keep every one else in that condition. We have forgotten, if we ever knew, that the best workers work, like God, "*ohne Hast, ohne Rast.*" We try to do more than we can do well. We fill every moment so full that it has no time to plan for the next moment, let alone for the next day. We have not learned the immense advantage of the long forward look. And so emergencies come upon us unprepared for. And so our lives are worn away in the fever of anxiety and fretting, and wear out other lives also, that without us might be more sensible.

Young men, young women, abolish from your vocabulary the words "rush" and "hurry up"! Be modest in the stints you set yourselves, be merciful in the stints you set others. Get into your lives the leisureliness of the eternal years, where there will be time for everything, just as there is in a well-ordered life on earth, and where no one will ever be known to "rush!" A thing is not worth hurrying after at all that would not be better gained without hurry. It is never worth while to live for the day unless at the same time we can live for all days.

CHAPTER XIV.

KEEPING PENCILS SHARP.

YOU can tell a great deal about a man by the way he cares for his pencil. This article always comes from some men's pockets with the neatest imaginable little tip,—just such a tip as the pencil-sharpener of an advertisement is pictured as putting on the pencil, but never can be induced to put on in reality except with the destruction of the lead. This pencil tip, in its beautiful symmetry and its business-like readiness for the next demand, is the despair of most men— and of all women, for the majority of us inefficient mortals chew our pencils into ragged ugliness, break the lead, or wear it down to the bone, and then slip our clerkly tool into our pocket, blissfully unconscious that there will ever be a next time when the pencil will be in demand.

A man who always keeps his pencil in good order is pretty certain to have some other valuable characteristics. In this little act he shows forethought for the future,—a prudence

that is likely to extend to greater matters.
The man whose motto is, "Sufficient unto the
hour is the pencil point thereof," will, if he
carries out that notion, spend his salary as rapidly as he gets it, use his strength to the utter-
most stretch of endurance, and lay in no sup-
ply for the mental and physical needs of to-
morrow or next year.

Whoever keeps his pencils sharp is likely to
have a proper regard for tools. He will probably brush his teeth regularly and thoroughly.
He may care for his nails, and for the rest of
that most marvellous of all tools, the human
hand. His books will not be dog's-eared. His
axe will have an edge, and his razor will
shave.

Moreover, if he cares properly for his pencil, it is probably because he intends to be
ready for emergencies. The man that has to
sharpen his pencil to get lead enough for an
entry in his memorandum-book will never be
ready with his tongue to oppose an unworthy
candidate when he is sprung upon the primary,
nor prepared with his wits to do the right
thing in an accident or at a fire.

Neatness in pencil, according to my observation, is attended by neatness in dress. A
sloven in any one particular is likely to be a
sloven in other and in many particulars. More-

over, accuracy in pointing a pencil is often ac-
companied, according to my observation, by
accuracy in speech and with the pen. And,
finally, patience has few better exemplifica-
tions than in the careful and painstaking sharp-
ening of one of these little cedar sticks.

From one thing learn all. A man's entire
character may be read even in his necktie, if
we have eyes to see. How much more may it
be read in his lead-pencil! One sure test of a
worker is his tools.

CHAPTER XV.

THE railroad on which I live made not long ago, at great expense, a decided improvement. For miles, where they had had only two tracks, they added two more. The outer tracks are used for the through traffic, that moves rapidly, and the inner tracks for the local trains, that must stop at every station.

You can see at once what an advantage this is. The fast trains are not obliged to choose between possible rear collisions or slowing down to the time of the locals. Freights can move more conveniently ; and when anything is the matter with one track, why, there are the others to fall back on.

Now I know people that could with great profit take a lesson from this railway. They run all their interests on one track, or two at the most. They do everything in the same way, at the same rate of speed. They deliberate as long over a friendly note as over a letter to the President. They study as long over the probable length of the judgeship of Barak as over the Ten Commandments. They sharpen a pencil as an artist would carve a statue.

You see what I mean. These are people that have no sense of proportion. They are equally thorough in everything, and never do the important things half as well as they should, just because they do the unimportant things twice as well as they should. They run no express trains, but all their trains are accommodation.

If these folks, now, had only four tracks to their lives, what a difference it would make! They would see that here is a matter whose value consists, not in its being done precisely as well as with time and the quiet use of all our powers we might be able to do it, but in being done *quickly*. They would put such things on the express tracks. They would see other matters that require deliberation and plodding painstaking. They would place these on the accommodation trains.

This is no slight matter. More and more in this whirling world success is won by those that know something about relative values,— what books to skim and what to read carefully, what speeches to write out and commit to memory and what to make off-hand, what bits of work to do only as well as the need requires and what to make master-pieces.

"Get a move on you," is one of the most expressive of the slang phrases of the day,—so expressive that I regret that it is slang. Possibly it will not be slang if I paraphase it to read, "Get several different moves on you." In other words, "Live four-tracked lives."

"But how about Solomon?" some of you want to ask. "Did he not tell us to do with our might what our hands find to do?"

Certainly ; and Solomon, as usual, is correct. To say, however, that Solomon in that sentence meant to urge equal thoroughness in all matters is to charge him with the opposite of wisdom, and even with a decided lack of common sense. Do you suppose Solomon spent as much time and thought in writing a letter to Hiram, king of Tyre, as in writing Ecclesiastes? The degree of thoroughness adequate for the one would have been very inadequate for the other. Do you imagine that he thought over as carefully what he was going to say at the first audience given the Queen of Sheba at the dedication of the temple?

No. Solomon would never have gained the world's love and admiration for his wisdom if he had not known how to divide his time fitly among his duties, assigning to each

their proper proportion of thought and attention.

"Do with your might what your hands find
to do," he urged, and most wisely. Put your
whole soul into everything you undertake.
Do everything well, and with enthusiasm.
But—and this is the point—don't do anything
too well ; don't put so much of your time and
energy into one thing that no time and
energy, or insufficient time and energy, are
left for matters which God would rather you
would do. To make a crate as carefully as
you would make a parlor cabinet is not thoroughness, but wastefulness.

If you could realize how many "thorough"
business men have no time to go to prayer
meeting, how many "thorough" letter-writers
have no time for reading their Bibles, how
many "thorough" housekeepers have no time
for the games and the merry cheer that would
soften and gladden and enrich their children's
lives and bind them forevermore to home—if
you could realize what crimes against God and
man are daily committed under cover of this
false thoroughness, you would eagerly join in
my protest against it.

Be thorough in everything,—yes, I can even
put it that way,—but recognize always various degrees of thoroughness, and give to each

pleasure and each task just the thoroughness that will keep it in its right relation to other pleasures and tasks, and you will be a thorough workman who needs not to be ashamed.

CHAPTER XVI.

VERY worker, doubtless, is sadly conscious that with respect to work there are two classes of days. On the first kind of day everything slips along as easily as a toboggan going down the slide. On the second kind of day everything gets sidetracked. At the close of days of the first kind you can reckon up a long list of accomplishments, and your immortal head collides with the stars. At the close of days of the second class you sorrowfully and ignominiously ask yourself, " What have I done to-day, anyway ? " and echo answers, " What ? "

Yet on the second days you are just as busy as on the first, only—you don't seem to do anything. It is like trying to go upstairs in a dream. It is like attempting to climb to the top of a tread mill. It gives you a sort of eerie feeling, when you stop to think of it. Are you bewitched ? Or are things bewitched ?

In reality it is neither. In reality probably you have been accomplishing just as much on one day as on another; that is, if you are a good worker. It will save you much needless depression, and the lack of efficiency that depression brings with it, if you will recognize two classes of days, equally necessary, equally fruitful, but far from equal in the show they make,—namely, getting-ready days and finishing days.

On the getting-ready days you hunt up your material; on the finishing days you write your article. On the getting-ready days you do your shopping; on the finishing days you make your dress. On the getting-ready days you straighten things out; on the finishing days you bring in the new sofa. More work is likely to be done on the getting-ready days than on the finishing days, but it is hidden under ground, like the foundation of a house. Did you ever know that builders consider a house half built when a good level foundation is laid? And yet people who look on, date the beginning of the building from the first course laid on the foundation.

And the point of application is, that we ought to distribute over the getting-ready days the satisfaction—or most of it—that attends the finishing days. We ought to recognize the foundation work as genuine accomplishment. Rightly considered, everything finished is only the beginning of something else, and all beginnings, as far as they go, are finished achievements. And to a worker who is under God's direction, and seeking only to do His will day by day, whether in the cellar or on the house-tops, getting-ready days and finishing days will be equally happy and equally successful.

CHAPTER XVII.

DOUBTLESS your friends heard you say, "Now I mean to buckle down to work," but doubtless also they have often watched you after this so-called buckling down, and have seen that you didn't even fasten yourself to your work with a double bow-knot,—nothing but a slip-knot, and a very poor one at that.

The virtue of a buckle is that by means of it you can get right tight hold of a thing, and keep tight hold. To a buckle there are three parts. In the first place there is a strap, which gives the buckle a long reach; then there is a frame, whereby the buckle gets a leverage; and finally there is a tongue or catch, whereby the buckle retains its hold on all that the strap gathers in through the leverage of the frame.

Now all this is a part of the parable which you unconsciously use when you declare that you mean to buckle down to your work. The strap of this work-buckle is the understanding of your work, which reaches all around it, and gives you a grasp on all sides of it. You can't buckle down to work if you know only the top of it. No buckle will hold on a task if you are acquainted with only one side of the task. No half-way man, no one-sided man, can in any real sense buckle down to his work, though, in good sooth, he can easily enough pretend to. The first third, then, of this operation of buckling down to one's work, consists in the application of the strap, the getting some all-round comprehension of the work and its requirements.

The second third is the frame. It is the spiritual leverage or purchasing power on the work. No one can buckle down to a task without will power, a bull-dog determination to do the work, come what may. The man of weak will throws off his coat, rolls up his sleeves, grits his teeth, and then—sits down in the shade to think about his work. The frame-work of the buckle doesn't say anything. It lets the bundle that is being grasped do the talking and the groaning, while it squeezes it. Thus the worker who buckles down to his work quietly goes ahead with persistent determination, and the work some way goes ahead with him.

But, after all, important as the grasp of the

strap and the leverage of the frame may be, it is the catch of the buckle that holds. Without that, however the strap may be tied and twisted, however stout the frame may be, the best buckle in the world is worthless. This tongue of the work-buckle is the tongue of prayer, whereby your strength is stayed by God's strength. In that case alone there is no slipping. In that case alone the widest reach of the most comprehensive purpose will hold good. In that case alone the firmest purchase of the most dogged will has no chance of losing what it gains.

The next time you promise yourself to buckle down to your task, bear in mind, then, these three factors of the metaphor ; and while you look on all sides of your work, and while you go at your task with vigor and energy, do not forget the little tongue of prayer that is to make it all taut and permanent.

CHAPTER XVIII.

"CAN" CONQUERS.

IT is said that Henry Ward Beecher considered that the best lesson he ever learned, he learned at school in the following way. He was sent to the board to do an example in arithmetic. When he had finished, the master looked at it and said, " Henry, you may do it again."

Henry did it again; but as before the teacher, after glancing at it, merely remarked, " Henry, you may do it again."

" I think it is right, sir," said the boy, " but I will try it once more."

The third time he tried it, and the third time the teacher merely said, " Henry, you may do it again."

" Why," said young Beecher, " the answer is right; I know it is right."

" Yes," replied the master, " *it has been right all the time*, but you did not know it was. Nothing is right to you until you know that it is right."

Much of the discipline of life is simply to teach us confidence in ourselves. We could save ourselves much of that discipline by recognizing our own powers, and adhering more faithfully to the truths God gives us. It is a great folly to be conceited and obstinate, but probably more young men are in danger of distrusting their own thoughts and methods, especially when they see that adherence to them puts them in the minority and makes them a laughing-stock. "Go back to your slate and your A B C," says the world to many an enterprising toiler; but the true worker, like Beecher the abolitionist, knows when he is right, and goes ahead from the decisive starting-point of that decision.

So much, in work, depends on the "state of mind" in which the worker is.

"It is just the way you feel," said the man in front of me in the car. "Now some days I know I won't make a strike"—they were evidently talking about bowling—"a strike or even a spare; and I don't. And then again, other days—don't you know?—I can feel it in my bones that I am going to hit 'em just right, and the ball spins right down the centre and knocks 'em every time. Why, I can tell before the ball leaves my hand whether it's going right or wrong. It's funny, isn't it? But I can." There was more of it, much more of it, for he was one of the men that say a thing over several times in as many different ways as they can think of; but he didn't *say* anything else.

What he had said, though, was enough to set me to thinking. Isn't it true of the great game of life, as it certainly is true of bowling, that the man who feels he is going to fail generally justifies his feelings, while the man who is confident of success comes out the champion? There are exceptions to all rules, but do we always realize how much of the battle is the spirit in which we enter it?

Skill counts; of course it does. No amount of confidence will gain a victory for a wretched bowler against a crack player. But when two are evenly matched, have you any doubt which will win, the one that believes in himself, or the one that distrusts himself?

A spent bullet, that will nestle harmlessly against a soldier's shirt, will nevertheless so stun him by the force of its impact that he must be carried from the field. A cannon-ball was once rolling quietly along the ground, seemingly ready to stop. A soldier tried to check it with his foot, and it broke his leg. Motion has in it a terrible power. Simply to be set going, and then to keep on going, will transform any dull block of stone or metal into a mighty engine.

There are some men that have caught the knack of this. " I never have failed," often says a young man we know, "and I do not propose to fail this time." Thus he gathers up all his past successes into a present momentum; and thus Emerson's noble line has become true of him, " His heart is the throne of will."

But—and this, alas! Emerson did not see— the young man's heart is the throne of will only because Christ is enthroned there. " I can do all things through Christ who strengtheneth me," is the young man's favorite motto, and in that sign he conquers.

In this way Christian confidence is reconcilable with Christian humility; for it is the Christian's duty to be confident, but it is his ruin to be *self*-confident. Momentum is always something impressed on matter from the outside; no cannon-ball can set itself to rushing through the air. " Do you expect to make any impression on the vast Chinese Empire?" they asked Morrison, the pioneer missionary to China. " No," was the grand reply, " but I expect that God will." And so was put in motion a cannon-ball that will yet batter down the great Chinese wall. The more we get of

God's spirit and power,—the more, in other words, God becomes ourselves,—the more we have a right to trust ourselves. When God is within, to trust ourselves is, in a true sense, to dishonor God.

"I can," then, must be our motto, brother workers, sister workers, and we dare let no weaker words pass our lips. The taps of a cork hammer, repeated regularly and long enough, will set to swinging an enormous mass of iron. Store up your little successes won through Christ, and soon their accumulated momentum will be irresistible. Do not admit for a second the possibility of failure; that would be to lose all you have gained; for the cannon-ball, if it stopped in its course and retreated only a sixteenth of an inch, would destroy all its momentum as surely as if it retreated a mile.

"Fear is dead! Fear is dead!" cry the Hindoos, dancing around the ugly clay image of the god; but some creep within the circle and kiss the statue's feet, lest Fear be not altogether dead, after all. How often we Christians imitate that heathen ceremony! Let us imitate it no longer. Let us advance to whatever work God appoints with the cry upon our lips, "God wills it! God wills it!" and with every step of our onward rush, motion will be changed to momentum, and it will be harder to check our progress, and this petty barrier and that will be tossed lightly aside, until at length, by the continued accretion of small victories, we shall have drawn to ourselves His power whose name is Victory, and all things will be possible to us, because we believe.

CHAPTER XIX.

PREPARED TO FAIL.

A MAN that works rightly, then, has a right to expect success; more than that, it is his duty to be confident. But we must set over against this a a complementary truth: the Christian worker who is prepared to fail is in a large measure prepared to succeed. This is true of no worker but a Christian worker. A man of the world can have little heart for his toil unless he expects to prosper in it. Forecast of failure is to him present despair and languor. Expectation of success is his necessary spur. It is said of the worldly worker that nothing succeeds like success. This is not true, even of him, but it is true of him that nothing succeeds like the expectation of success. This is because the zeal of the worldly worker is not from within, but from without; born not of the work itself, but of the work's reward.

Now the zeal of Christ's workmen is of the Spirit and not of the success, of the work and not of the result. His Master is not like the

masters of worldlings, that measure approval
by accomplishment; but his Master looks on
the heart. And so it happens that the spirit
of confidence which in the worldling's under-
takings is most necessary, is seen by the spiritually minded man to be actually a peril.

In Christian work almost everything depends on throwing the emphasis where it be-
longs, on pleasing God, just as in worldly work
it must be thrown, as worldlings think, on
pleasing men. And nothing is more pleasing
to God than the zealous surrender of our wills.
This is far from the abject, inane, Buddhistic
reduction of humanity to nothingness. It is
the elevation of humanity, rather, so near to
God that we will God's will, however it may
cross our lower desires.

And this is the last grace the Christian
worker wins, his crowning glory. When he
begins to work for Christ the results he seeks
seem so necessary and noble that the collapse
of the universe must follow his failure. After
long trial and many tears and much rebellious
doubting of God's providence, he begins to see
that God fulfills Himself in many ways, and in
ways too vast for his comprehension. Upon
the ruin of his labor God serenely builds more
grandly than he had planned. His human
failures are cheerily converted into divine suc-

cesses. And all this, as he comes to see, is not because God wishes exultingly and tantalizingly to prove His own superiority over men, but simply because God loves His workmen and His work too well to let them spoil each other.

Blessed be God that He uses us at all! that He grants to us clumsy blunderers a share in His vast building. Blessed be God that He loves us for our willingness to serve, and not for our success in service. Blessed be God that He permits us to fail—for Him!

CHAPTER XX.

THE SHOEMAKER AND HIS LAST.

I KNOW of a man who, in spite of the fact that he receives a good salary, insists on doing almost everything for which other men hire outside help. He runs his own garden, spending more for fertilizers than he ever gets from it in vegetables, and putting in his time at hard work after office hours, when it should have been put in at play. He beats his own carpets, leaving half the dust in them, and giving himself such a backache that he is fit for nothing at his regular work next day. He does his own carpenter work, botching every job. He mends his own pans and kettles,—so that they leak almost as badly as ever. He does his own plumbing,—until things get into such shape that he has to spend twice as much on the regular plumber as he would have spent if he had called him at first. He doctors his children as long as he dares, handing over to the physician aggravated cases every time. He regrets that he hasn't a shoemaker's outfit,

so that he might imitate his grandfather of
"the good old days," and cobble the family
shoes. He prides himself on being able, as he
expresses it, to "turn his hand to anything,"
and he calmly forgets that the clock he cleaned
has stopped forever, and the piano he tuned is
the terror of the neighborhood, and the new
carpet he put down looks like a bird's-eye view
of Switzerland.

The days when men did practically everything for themselves are passed, and happily
passed. It is better for men in this, as in other
respects, that they should not live alone, that
they should not live unto themselves. When
each man does his proper work, the work for
which he has a native skill coupled with an
adequate training and experience, and calls on
others to do their proper work for him,
then all work is done in the shortest time and
in the best way. The shoe is more neatly
cobbled, then, and really at less cost. The
garden brings a profit, then, and the dress fits,
and the carpet lies smooth and lasts longer.

Besides, for most men, there is a most important side to this question,—their duty to
their employers. Statute law may not touch
the case, but what moral law permits a man,
who has sold his strength and talents to another for an agreed salary, to spend his

strength and talents in ways detrimental to the work he has agreed to do?

I have seen clerks so sedulous up to midnight in cultivating their musical talents in an amateur orchestra that they could scarcely keep their eyes open next day to wait upon customers.

I have seen teachers so devoted to their flower-garden that they gave far more attention to their tulips and their roses than to their boys and girls.

I have seen preachers—I would not call them by the sacred name of *ministers*—more bent on bicycling than on the saving of souls.

Workers, you cannot improve Paul's motto: "This *one* thing I do." You cannot afford to spread yourselves over more ground than Paul. This advice does not preclude doing many things. Work to the top of your powers, and you will not be likely to work in half as many difficult ways as that mighty apostle, missionary, preacher, evangelist, scholar, traveller, writer, and tent-maker. The advice *does* require, however, that all your diversified occupations have a common centre and aim. That aim, for you, as for Paul, is the work, whatever it is, that God has given you to do.

About this let all things cluster. To this

let all things minister. To do it best you must play, but play only enough to do it best. To do it best you must mingle socially with men, but only enough so that you may do it best. To do it best you must cultivate your musical talents, perhaps, or your talents for writing, or speaking, or painting, or cooking doughnuts,—but only enough to do it best.

And this is the only way to keep your life from confusion, and fretfulness, and failure.

CHAPTER XXI.

T is great fun on "my" railroad,—that is, the road enriched by my daily twenty cents, to notice the different ways the different brakemen take of calling out the stations reached, or next to be reached. Some will wait till the very last minute, when, amid the final jar of the cars as the engine slackens its speed, they will throw open the door and bawl out, "Cogefum," for "Cottage Farm," or "Nunvul" for "Newtonville." When the train takes up its course again, they slam the door with another fierce scream, "Nestay Aundle," which, being interpreted, is, "Next station, Auburndale."

Some brakemen are evidently in the last stages of consumption, and feebly whisper their announcements. Some are thick-tongued, and put unavailing vigor into what might just as well be Choctaw. Some drawl out their calls as if they were pulling a long rope of molasses candy. Some clip off their calls as if every word were cayenne pepper.

98

There is one brakeman on my road, however, who delights my heart whenever I am fortunate enough to catch his train. He closes the door quietly, advances into the middle of the car, and sings out cheerfully and with perfect distinctness, "The next station is Allston." This having been accomplished, he retires with great dignity.

Every time this happens, I feel like getting up and saying to the young men in the car: "Gentlemen, there has just been enacted before you a parable of success. That brakeman is not afraid to do more than his duty. He magnifies his office, and I shall be greatly surprised if his office does not magnify him. He ought to be a conductor right away, and, as soon thereafter as possible, superintendent of the road. Yes, he ought. He does more than the contract calls for. He gives good measure, pressed down and running over. He takes pride in his work. He rounds off the corners and putties up the cracks. Be such a clerk, young man, as he is a brakeman, or such a typesetter, or bookkeeper, or teacher, or stenographer, or what not, and success is yours. Be ——."

But before that sentence, probably, they would have put me off the train.

CHAPTER XXII.

HERE are some people who, before they go on very far in life, discover that they are more expensive than other folks. Their teeth are of the crumbling kind, whose caverns become regular gold mines, of the reverse order. Their eyes have so many twists that the fullest pocket-book gets the cramps trying to fit them with glasses. Their tender feet raise a corn on every toe as a red flag of rebellion against leather that is not of the finest and shoes that are not of the shrewdest make.

O, they are to be pitied, these expensive folk! Ordinary, cheap food is poison to their unreasonable stomachs. Ready-made, cheap clothing is offensive to their fastidious taste. Their sensitive, accurate ears shrink from anything but the finest pianos, and violins worth many times their weight in gold. A tawdry, paper-covered book, with inartistic type,— pah! they'd rather not read at all than read that. Ugly wall-paper drives them out of doors. Ingrain carpets are nettles under their feet. Better is a slice of bread at Delmonico's than a plate of turkey at Mrs. Smith's boarding-house. Worst of all, their constitutions are so delicately adjusted that their work must fit them as a glove the finger, must give precisely the right surroundings, the right hours, the right amount of freedom and leisure, or they are unable to work at all.

And so it happens that where others are large and liberal producers, these are chiefly consumers. If they are rich, they are idle and miserable; and if they are poor, they pose as martyrs at the very toil wherein others are singing. In neither case is the world the richer for them, either in goods or good cheer. They were born to be expensive.

No, that is not true. God did not create them to be expensive. God is not such a bungling workman as that would indicate. God makes no mistakes. To be sure, He may have sent the misshapen eyes and the chalky teeth and the dyspeptic stomach and the tender feet and the delicate sensibilities,—matters which are expensive enough; but He always sends far more possibilities of wealth than sources of poverty.

Listen, ye poor myopic, astigmatic, æsthetic, dyspeptic, rack-eared, plug-toothed unfortunates! Hear a word of common sense from a plain thinker. More can come out of a man than ever need go into him. If you are expensive above the ordinary, be productive above the ordinary. Make up for the gold mine stowed away in your teeth by those words fitly spoken, that are like apples of gold in silver baskets. Pay for your complex and costly eye-glasses by using your eyes in some unique and valuable fashion. Get as much out of your dyspeptic body—in your way—as Carlyle got out of his, in his way. Must your feet be daintily shod? Speed them on the swifter errands. Are your tastes refined, accurate, sensitive? Fall to, with your trained love of beauty, and beautify this old world, instead of grumbling at it.

There's a noble work for every one. There's a wealth-producing work for every one,—wealth of spirit, and wealth of the United States mint as well. And let every child of God that appropriates largely of God's good things bestir himself, with God's help, to pay back even more than he takes. No such endeavor can end in failure.

CHAPTER XXIII.

PEOPLE THAT MEAN BUSINESS.

YOUNG friend of mine has lately moved from a little country town to the great city of Boston. In the little country town where he had spent his life everything went on in easy, humdrum fashion, much the same, day after day; no one ever too busy to stop and chat; a place where it was rather respectable than otherwise to have nothing to do, provided one paid his debts. "Now," thought that young man, "I know something of cities. I have seen Chicago and New York and other bustling, egotistic towns; but Boston the learned, Boston the sedate, will be much like my little country village, only bigger."

Arrived, he found streets more crowded than he ever saw streets before; and crowded with men more intent on business than he ever saw men before, darting along like confused swarms of dodging arrows, each with an air which seemed to say, "Keep to your own side of the sidewalk. Don't get in my way. I

mean business!" The shades of those quiet
spirits, Emerson, Hawthorne, Lowell, Longfellow, Alcott, Mann, which he expected to
see still haunting their old peaceful walks,—
he saw no room for these calm ghosts. Boston
was a hive of bees which meant business, not
a drone among them; or if drones were there,
they hid their faces in shame in the depths of
the hive.

Well, this young friend of mine, after he
had got over his surprise, was pleased with it
all. It was an inspiration to get into a place
where every one had something to do, and
was in earnest about doing it. He rather en-
joyed being hustled to one side by energetic
men. It gave him energy to shoulder some
one else out of the way. He was glad to get
into a place where people meant business.

But he was not long in Boston before he
began to modify this opinion. He soon came
across folks whose business was chiefly brag and
bustle. They snapped every string. They
pulled tighter every knot. They burst every
button. They split every box. They tripped
over their own feet. They talked so much
that they said nothing. They did so much
that they did nothing. And very soon, in
talking about people that mean business he
learned to explain that he did not mean *them*.

Nor was he in Boston much longer without still further limiting the phrase. He learned that many folks mean business spasmodically. To-day there is nothing so fine in all the world as the task in which they are engaged. Every energy shall be given to it. It deserves a life's devotion, and it shall have it. Hip, hip, hooray for it! To-morrow,—yawns, groans, fidgets. Things are not so fine as they appeared at first. Work is too hard. Pay is inadequate. Probably another field would be better. No, my young friend from the country soon decided that these people did not mean business.

Still later he came across another class of business men. These people did seem buried in business. They were wrapped up in it as in a shroud, so that they walked the streets like corpses and rode in the cars as if the cars were hearses. They were deaf to all sounds but those of their business, and blind to all sights except those of their occupations. They seemed to mean business in earnest. But my young friend soon perceived that all business is so closely linked to the world of manifold activity around it that no man can comprehend his business without some close acquaintance with that world. He found that the quickest way to kill one's business is to bury one's self in it. And so my young friend had to make another exception.

Yet once more, after still longer acquaintance with business men, this lad of ours discovered a fourth spurious class. These folks were harder to detect, because they were bright and sensible in their business ways, not spasmodic, not mere bustle, not buried in business, but wide awake and enterprising. But my young friend found out that these people meant business only so long as business meant gain for them, and ease, and popularity. Their business was based on self. It helped no one else, designedly, at least. It had no ends of common welfare. They were ready to drop it like hot coals at any instant when it ceased to minister to themselves. These people, my young man concluded, do not really mean business.

But he did find some folks that could not be denied the title—the proud title—of business men. Who were they? Do you know of one of old who said, "Wist ye not that I must be about My Father's business?" Well, they were people like Him. They were calm, bright-eyed people, who did not jostle others, or knit their brows, or walk the street like mummies in their cases. They were deeply interested in their work, only it was because it was not their work, but their Father's. Because it was His, they never worried about it; He would care for His own. But because it was His, they put their whole lives heartily into it. These people, my friend decided, were true business men. They did mean business, cheerily, nobly, divinely; because business meant so much to them.

CHAPTER XXIV.

WHERE TO WORK.

EW young men,—and nowadays we must add "young women,"—on starting out in their business or professional life, realize the immense advantage of beginning at home, especially if their home is in a country town or a small city. The big, bustling metropolis swims before their dazzled eyes as a very paradise of opportunity. They read stories of the rapid rise of this millionaire or that, stories which may be true or not, but which are sure to leave out all the discouragements and difficulties, and which forget to mention the fact that since our present millionaires were boys the business world has so changed that methods which brought them enormous wealth might to-day prove but a byway to bankruptcy.

It is my decided judgment that the young man who gets his business training at home has a chance for advancement when he goes to the city many times greater than the city boy, and it is merely because I do not wish just here

to enter upon another topic that take it for
granted that he must go to the city at all. To
be sure, he may spend years on a salary lower
than his city cousins. He may fret and worry
over the "slow ways" and the "picayune policy" of his country associates in trade. He
may feel that every week a thousand glorious
opportunities are slipping by him. But if he
has the right material in him, if he has a
clear head and a sound heart, if he possesses
grit and originality and tact, his apprenticeship in the country or in the small town is
coining the dollars of his future fortune.

There he is known; in the city he would be
unknown. There he is somebody; in the city
he would be nobody. There he has the proud
consciousness—more or less justified—that he
is well toward the top; in the city he would
be discouraged by the enormous mass of
mortals on top of him. There his originality
is unfettered; in the city he must make of his
life a cog fitting exactly into the great, whirling cog-wheel. There he has room and can
expand naturally; in the city he can scarcely
breathe without inhaling second-hand air.
There everybody takes an interest in him.
They may insult his dignity by calling him
Jack, but he is the Jack whose baby form they
have dangled on their knees, or whose father

was their best friend at school. In the city he would be " You," or " No. 52," or " That Jones." In the country his little successes are the property and the pride of the entire community. They get into the village paper. The small boys point him out. In the city,— well, his boarding-house has a rather transient population, that's a fact.

I could keep up this sort of contrast for some time, for I am full of the subject; but you see the point. Stay where you are known, young men. Get your experience at home. It will be good experience. It will come ten-fold easier than in the city. It will develop in you confidence and a courageous manliness, while the city would be crushing all the confidence out of you and all the good cheer, and changing you from a man into that thing called a pessimist. And if, after some good, solid years of this, you have a fair chance of carrying into the city's whirl your freshness and your buoyancy and your fine country sprightliness and sturdy good sense, they will be quoted at par in its markets, never fear. For character counts, and courage counts, and ability finds a place for itself, and your life, through this natural, quiet, simple progress, has been building into its structure these three supreme qualifications of all success.

So much for the start; now a word about new situations and when to take them.

A very noble story is told of President Anderson of Rochester University. He was offered the presidency of Brown University,—a most enviable position, and one especially attractive to him. But he declined it, and on quite unusual grounds, for he said: "Go? No, I am going to stand by Rochester. Rochester invested in me when I was unknown and without value; if the investment has not proved a failure, Rochester deserves the profits."

How many men, helped to start in life, consider the firm or the institution that has given them this start as merely a stepping-stone on which they may climb to what they falsely think higher things! They call that "bettering" themselves, when they really, by their disregard of the first principles of gratitude and honor, have cheapened themselves and their eternal life.

A dealer in paper was talking to me not long ago. "I could save to *The* ——," said he, referring to one of the leading journals of the country, "many thousands of dollars a year if they would buy their paper of me rather than of the firm with which they are dealing, but they will not hear of such a thing. You see, when

the owner of *The* —— was starting the paper,
sixty years ago, this paper firm had confidence
in him, and trusted the young man to any extent, though he had no money to pay his paper
bills for some years. And now do you think
that any saving would induce the proprietor
of *The* —— to withdraw his patronage from
that firm ? No, sir !"

The right thing for a young man to do when
tempted to leave the employ of a firm he respects, and to which he owes his initial chance
in this world, is first to consider whether there
is any moral reason why he should not remain
with that firm all his life, and if there is not,
to decide to put into his position there so much
zeal and faithfulness as to make it worth to
him and the world all that he could hope to
gain from *any* position that he could expect to
open to him elsewhere.

To make one's position twice as valuable as
it is now is tenfold better than stepping out
from it into another position twice as valuable.
Strike your roots deep, workers, and grow
where you are.

And permit me a few remarks, in conclusion,
on the choice of easy situations. This world
is full of soft heads looking for soft jobs.
What is a soft job ? It is one that puts hard
cash into soft hands. It is one that gives for

the least amount of work the greatest amount
of pay. A job that you can sublet at a big
profit, a job that offers sure pay for lucky hits,
a job that calls for one who is good-looking
rather than good for something,—these are
soft jobs. Ah, the woods are full of men
hunting them.

Now, there are several reasons why I should
fight shy of such jobs, if I were you, young
men. In the first place, a soft job is almost
certain to make a hard heart. No one can
sympathize with this world's toilers and suffer-
ers who is not toiling and suffering with them.
Those that have soft jobs are sure to be snobs.

In the second place, a soft job means a soft
brain. Brains are toughened by hard work,
not by soft work. If you have to bend your
minds fiercely and constantly upon some
worthy task, they find in it a philosopher's
stone to turn them to gold. If you exercise
your minds upon bubbles, they also become
gassy.

But finally, a soft job means hard luck. It
does, indeed. Reflect that when hard times
come it is the men with the soft jobs that have
to go. The men who are giving money's worth
for money, and they alone, are assured of keeping their places very long.

Honest, solid work for honest, unextravagant pay, the weary body at night and the cheery song in the morning, a little home where love dwells, and a hearth aglow with contentment,—seek no softer job than that, workers, if you want happiness in this world and the next.

CHAPTER XXV.

WHAT IS UNDER YOUR HEAD?

I HAVE an important question to propound to every worker. As I ask it, you may fancy, if you will, that I am a regular Sphinx, sitting along the road named Success in Life, and turning off on the gloomy bypath of Disappointment every one of you that cannot answer my question satisfactorily. You'd better heed it now, as it comes from my harmless self, and be prepared to make a good answer when you are cross-examined, as you surely will be, by the Sphinx of This World.

But I have been rambling on as if you knew what the awful question is. I will whisper it. Listen :

What is under your head ?

What are you laughing at, my giddy readers? That's a solemn question, I tell you, when asked as that Sphinx asks it, with her great paw ready to knock you off to one side unless you answer it well.

115

But you don't know what the question means? All the worse for you, if you have done so little thinking about what is under your head that you do not at once catch the import of such a query.

First (as the Sphinx will want to know). Is a good pair of lungs under your head? Brains are fine things, with their wise wrinkles and sage convolutions; but brains, after all, are dull things without lungs to blow the breath of life into them, and keep it there, fresh and vigorous. Why, your brain may be as big as Cuvier's or Butler's, but if your lungs are as shrivelled as some must be, I would no more insure your intellectual fame than a life-insurance company would insure your poor, ill-treated body.

Secondly. Is a good stomach under your head? You may laugh, but just wait until you try to drive genius and dyspepsia in the same harness. Brains and bile are mortal foes. If your stomach won't digest food, it really doesn't matter how many tons of facts your brains will digest. A strong head on a weak stomach is about as useful as the Lick telescope would be planted on a bobbing buoy.

Thirdly. Is a good pair of hands under your head? Not hands white and delicately formed, though I have no objection in the world to that; but—what is more to the point in connection with your head—hands that are shrewd to carry out what the brain is shrewd to contrive, busy hands, accurate hands, quick hands, ready hands, gentle hands, brave hands, —are those under your head? Hands that can write down your brain's wise fancies with a penmanship clear as print. Hands that can, if need be,—and need is likely to be,—help your fine brain eke out a livelihood. A brain without hands is like a general without staff officers.

Fourthly. Is a good pair of feet under your head? Not feet that are weak and clumsy, and smarting with corns, and—pretty because the tightly squeezed leather outside is pretty, but feet that retain nature's beautiful outlines, feet that are on good terms with the ground, and can press it with loving, easy grace, for a happy twenty miles at a time. Errand-speeding feet. Dancing, springing, merry feet. Feet soft and light in sick-rooms. Feet sturdy and swift on the path of duty. Are these under your head?

O, I know what a masterful thing a head is. I know what mountain-high difficulties it can overleap. I know what triumphs a Henry Martyn, for instance, can wring out of his frail, fever-tortured, cough-racked body, "burning out for God." I know that when God chooses to hold up a man's head with nothing under it,—or next to nothing, like Mahomet's coffin suspended in mid-air by invisible forces,—God can do it. But. just the same, He seldom does do it; and it is the most impudent presumption to abuse our bodies in the faith that He will do it.

Look upon your head, young people,—and old,—as the glorious climax of your body; but don't try to build a pyramid out of an apex, with no foundation. In one sense, the pedestal is as important as the statue that it supports. And if your pedestal is crumbling, and just ready to totter, stop your chiselling away at the statue long enough to build up a stout pedestal, else the statue itself, with all its growing beauty, will topple in ruin to the ground.

CHAPTER XXVI.

E have gone a long way into our work when we have wisely begun it.

In that delicious book, " The Peterkin Papers," Solomon John decides to become a great writer. So the family hunts up some sheets of paper, manufactures ink from berries, chases a hen and makes a quill pen. Paper spread out, new pen dipped solemnly in the ink, awed family standing in expectancy, Solomon John suddenly discovers that he has nothing to write!

How like Solomon John do we often start into our work! We propose to make wonderful progress. But in what direction? We expect to improve. Improve what? We shall reach the goal in triumph. What goal?

Would we start on a voyage as we start into a day, a month, or a year? No. We should have definite aims, know the best ship, understand the dangers of the trip, take out an accident insurance policy, study the route.

Do men start thus in business? No. They

119

take account of their capital, watch their risks, study the state of the market, note their chances for gain.

Why, we plunge into most of our work as rash boys dive into strange waters—eyes shut, hands over heads, and down we go! No wonder that we sometimes bring sharply up against stones.

How the proverbs cry out against us! "Foresight is better than insight." "A stitch in time saves nine." "Prevention is better than cure." "Well warned is half armed."

I used to be drilled by a shrewd sergeant, one of whose tricks was the command, "Make ready—take aim—" and then would come a pause, during which some impatient gun would be certain to go off. "Vy don't you vinish aiming?" growls the sergeant.

Take good aim, every day, before you fire into your work. Stop right here, and think. Do you want to begin this day where you began last, or where you left off? If the latter, think over the experiences yesterday brought you. What did it show to be your special temptations? What helps did you find most beneficial? And where are you faulty now? Select one point for improvement, and only one. Do not aim too high, or too low. Do not try to do more than you can, or less.

Shall it be your temper, your bashfulness, your inaccuracy, your slowness? Whatever it be, "make ready,—*take a good, long aim,—* FIRE!"

The brute lives in the moments, a life of disconnected dots. So does the brute-like man. For him the past has no stimulus and no warning. the future no invitation. But the life of the wise man is a line, with a purpose in it, directed by what lies behind, and aiming well at something ahead. Paul forgot the things that were behind, he said, and pressed on to things that lay before him; but we can be sure he never let go of the past till it had yielded up to him its last drop of instruction and blessing.

How can you tell the ignorant laborer and the skilled mechanic? The first goes about his tasks with an air of monotonous plodding, one day's work like another's, with no sense of possible progress. The second looks eagerly at what he has done, with an eye trained to note defects and beauties, and a brain quick to see how the next piece of work may be free from these defects and increase these beauties. This last is the only kind of work that grows, and work that grows is the only work that endures. Aimless repetition of tasks means death as much as aimless idleness means it. There is such a thing as stagnation in work.

God's labor is permanent in its results be cause it looks before and after, is cumulative, has its solid foundations and its spires of desire. And if we wish our life-work to have any measure of the firmness and success of God's great works, it must be made, like His, to grow with reasonableness out of the past, and look with purpose toward the years to come. There are no times so appropriate for this wise and linking meditation as the beginnings and endings of things—the start, when purpose has action, all fresh and unsullied, before it ; the close, when reason has action, with its lessons and promptings, behind it.

And yet, if we are already in the midst of affairs upon which we have entered with no thought of whether they are a worthy continuance of the past and lead toward a worthy future, it is best to stop in the midst of things ; and as the surveyor stations his instrument between the stake just passed and the new one to be set, so let our workman consider whether his life is in line with the best in his past, and with his purest hopes. If not, he can retrace his steps with thanksgiving for a great escape. If it is, he will plod on with a glad confidence that will more than pay for the loss of time.

Many workers seem afraid thus decisively to plan their work. Probably the wittiest of all the world's witty proverbs is this, which has come to us from the Germans: "The road to hell is paved with good intentions." In Italy and France and Portugal they have it that Satan's realm itself has the same sort of paving. Now this is the worst kind of lie —a half truth ! For though many a person has slipped on a shabbily-laid intention-stone and fallen, yet we may lay these paving-stones of good resolutions so firmly that they will become for us the very gold of the celestial streets.

For the Chinese are right when they say, " Be resolved, and the thing is done !" Have you ever heard that abominable proverb for which the Germans, again, are responsible, " A bad beginning makes a good ending " ? Never believe it, never ! When the Germans are wiser they cry, " Beginning and ending shake hands ! " Which is about what the Dutch saying means : " So begun, so done."

I do not like the way our common proverbs sneer at promises. " Promises are like pie-crust, made to be broken." " Promises fill no sack." " In the land of promise a man may die of hunger." " Fair promises bind fools." " A great many shoes are worn out before a man does what he says." " Promises and undressed cloth are apt to shrink." Four diferent nations gave us these ugly maxims, and I hope America will never coin such crabbed proverbs!

No, promises do make progress; resolutions make reform; good intentions pay good interest! "Everything is difficult at first," says John Chinaman, and when we have to make one of these difficult beginnings, of a trade, or a lesson, or a year, making a little promise to one's self does for the spirit what clinching one's teeth does for the body. It doesn't accomplish any of the work, but it braces us, and makes us more vigorous for our task.

Never mind if it does seem hard. Begin, any way. "Everything must have a beginning," say the proverbs of half of Europe, and the French and Italians add this noble saying: "For a web begun, God sends thread." Begin, that you may know with surprise and pleasure the truth of the words which the old Greek farmer-poet Hesiod once wrote, and which have become a proverb of all lands: "The beginning is half the whole."

Two cautions. Make no promise carelessly. Remember the proverb, "He who resolves suddenly, repents at leisure." Heed these wise words of stout Warwick: "I will forethink what I will promise, that I may promise but what I will do."

And resolve few things. "Who begins much, finishes little," say the Germans and Italians. "Promise little, and do much."

Most of all, if your paving-stones are not to lead you the wrong way, repeat to yourself the French proverb, "He is not done who is beginning." "Everything new is beautiful," remark the Italians, while the Germans add sarcastically, " The beginning and the end are seldom alike." Now " it is good to begin well, but better to end well." " The end crowns the work." Do not forget that.

So let us, as the Scotch say, "set a stout heart to a steep hillside." Practice the Chinese teaching, " Resolution is independent of age, but without it one lives a hundred years in vain." And heed the German warning, " He who does not improve to-day, will grow worse to-morrow."

CHAPTER XXVII.

HEAPING IT ON.

KNOW many overworked men. People come to them, begging them to make speeches, lead meetings, attend meetings, be on committees, and do numberless such jobs, and when they say, "I have already more work than I ought to do, and you really must excuse me," the faces of the pleaders light up with a sudden inspiration,—it is always the same smile, and you may always know just what is coming.— and they always say, "Why, if you had nothing to do I should not want you, but it is the people who are busiest that find most time to do things." And then they look for an instant capitulation.

I have heard that statement made so many, many times that I am moved to expostulate. Why should the work a man is doing be considered a warrant for putting more work upon him? Why should his compliance once, subject him to ceaseless requests that continue until he is driven into nervous prostration, or until he gets mad?

We don't treat the beasts in that way. When a horse has all he ought to pull, a driver does not say, " Now this horse has proved that he will pull. Let us heap on a ton more."

We don't treat in that way even the insensate earth. We don't fill our garden with twice as much seed as it ought to contain, and say, " If this were not good soil, I should not be putting my seeds in it ; but ground that has done the most, can always find strength to do more."

No: we believe in rest—for horses. We believe in fallow seasons—for soil. But for *men* we say, " The busiest man is the one to go to, if you want anything done."

Now, that is shrewd. The man who is hard at work all his life knows, of course, how to work well and quickly. When we have a job we naturally take it to the best workman.

Besides, " *noblesse oblige* " ; it is God who has given the workman his power to work, and God requires that the workman shall use his power to the best advantage. To a certain extent we are working with God when we show a good workman a chance for some useful service.

But, with all due regard for both these considerations, let us remember that we are our brothers' keepers,—keepers of our brothers' health as well as keepers of our brothers' souls. Before we even suggest any fresh tasks to a hard-working man, it is our duty to consider first whether he has not already as much as we have any right to expect him to do.

But why cannot the man himself refuse, if he really has not time? In the first place, a hard-working man is always good-natured. Then, too, such a man is almost certain to overestimate his strength. Besides, it is a very disagreeable thing to do, this constantly refusing requests to help in good works, especially when each of the requests asks for some quite little thing, though altogether they amount to a heavy undertaking. Such constant refusals hurt a man's temper, spoil his self-respect, and injure the work he is doing.

No. Be solicitous, if you will, that the *lazy* people get their fair amount of work. Set *them* to leading meetings. Appoint *them* on committees. Appeal to *them* in emergencies in your business life, your church work, your social work. Seek to equalize burdens, if you will. Take them off the backs that are heaped up mountain high, and put some of them on the backs that are now going scot-free. But never, *never* say, "That man is bravely bearing a noble load. Go to; let us put a straw upon it."

CHAPTER XXVIII.

TIME, THE WORKER'S GOLD MINE.

UPPOSE that as, one by one, you came to need your hours, each were brought to you, a shining substance wrapped in finest silk, borne by a glittering angel! Suppose that, if the angel delayed, you would lapse into unconsciousness, and if he tarried too long, you would pass out into death. How you would value time! How grateful you would be for its unfailing regularity, for the lavish fullness of the royal gift!

And if, at the close of each day, some angel should spread out before you a great book wherein had been written, with ink that could not fade, opposite each minute given you that day, the use you had made of it, how careful you would be in your expenditure of that priceless dower—time!

God does not send angels with hours wrapped in silk; He does better than that. With His own kind, invisible hand, He pours them out for you Himself. No such book as I have imagined exists, but a book more startling; for

your use of every instant of time is written
down in the body you carry around with you.
The way your fingers move is a chapter of
your life history. The quality of your glance
is a compact account of many an hour. Your
bearing, the tone of your voice, the color of
your skin, the curve of your mouth, all these
are epitomes of your time.

If this is true, it should be to every soul a
most solemn question, "What am I doing with
this sacred gift?" The answer to this question will fairly determine your life. As that
great man, William Ewart Gladstone, once
said, "Thrift of time will repay you with a
usury of profit beyond your most sanguine
dreams, and the waste of it will make you
dwindle, alike in intellectual and in moral
stature, beyond your darkest reckonings."

Out of the same bit of meat an eagle will
organize swiftness, and a snail, slowness; a
lion, fierceness; a snake, treachery; and a dog,
affection. So out of the same time some men
will build failures, and others, successes.

When Joseph Cook was in the seminary, the
boys often had to wait for dinner at their
boarding-house. He always spent that little
time over a dictionary in the corner of the
room. Dickens was able to accomplish so
much because, when he worked, he labored in-

tensely, and when he played, he played with all his heart. We admit to our lives too many neutral moments of time, moments when we are doing nothing in particular, and those neutral moments color the others.

Our American manufacturers are acknowledged to succeed largely because of their attention to the by-products, the so-called waste material. That has been the secret of all successful lives: they have recognized the supreme importance of five minutes. The time you waste in railroad stations, on the cars, at your dressing, over your newspaper, waiting in barber-shops, and the like, would serve, if you kept a wise book ready to your hand, to render you a learned man. Ten minutes wasted every day means, in a working life of fifty years, an entire year of 350 days, with eight working hours to each. "There is a time," says the Bible, "to every purpose under the heaven," but no time for the *purposeless.* The same young woman that can find no time for Ruskin has ample time for Conan Doyle.

It is when we come to take this large look over time, that our use of it appears in its most serious aspect. When we come to understand even a little of what eternity means, and of how intimately it is bound up with the passing minute, we see how well it must pay to treat

God generously with the time He gives us. To say, in effect, that we are so busy that we have no time for our Father's business,—no time for our Bible or for the quiet hour, no time for the Christian Endeavor topic or the Sunday-school lesson or church-work,—is to condemn ourselves as the most shortsighted of creatures.

It would be appropriate to quote here a rhyme I once wrote, which the editor of *Harper's Weekly* was kind enough to print :

"There was an old fellow who never had time
   For a fresh morning look at the Volume sublime ;
   Who never had time for the soft hand of prayer
   To smooth out the wrinkles of labor and care ;
   Who could not find time for that service most sweet
   At the altar of home where the dear ones all meet ;
   And never found time with the people of God
   To learn the good way that the fathers have trod ;
        But he found time to die ;
            O yes !
        He found time to die.

This busy old fellow, too busy was he
   To linger at breakfast, at dinner or tea,
   For the merry small chatter of children and wife,
   But led in his marriage a bachelor life.
   Too busy for kisses, too busy for play,
   No time to be loving, no time to be gay,
   No time to replenish his vanishing health,
   No time to enjoy his swift gathering wealth,
        But he found time to die ;
            O yes !
        He found time to die.

"This beautiful world had no beauty for him,
  Its colors were black, and its sunshine was dim.
  No leisure for woodland, for river or hill,
  No time in his life just to think and be still,
  No time for his neighbors, no time for his friends,
  No time for those highest immutable ends
  Of the life of a man who is not for a day,
  But, for worse or for better, for ever and aye.
          Yet he found time to die?
              O yes!
          He found time to die."

That is a suggestive phrase we use in regard to the employment of our odd moments,
—we say we are " putting in time." Putting
in time! Putting it in *what?*

Well, in the first place, we put this time into
the bank of character. Tell me how you employ your odd moments, and I will tell you
whether you are becoming wiser or more ignorant, stronger or weaker, more industrious or
more slothful. Any bank cashier knows that
the greater part of the capital of the world
consists not of the large deposits, but of the
little accounts of comparatively poor men. It
is these small accounts, regularly added to,
that make the backbone of the world's wealth.
Similarly, it is the little bits of time that make
the backbone of character.

These bits of time, when you " put them in,"
are put into your assets of power. The

strength of a tree is not gained, much of it, at the times when it seems to be doing most, putting out leaves, and parading flowers and fruits. It builds itself up in bulk and stamina during the times when it does not seem to be doing much of anything. Nature knows how to " put in " the odd moments. She knows how to " put in time." If your assets of power consist only of what you have gained by occasional splendid spurts, you are practically bankrupt.

And then, when you " put in time," you put it into a permanent fund of satisfaction, payable on demand. What a joy it is to be able to look back upon days and years spent thoroughly well, the chinks all filled with useful work and useful play ! I know of no higher worldly joy than this, and the joy is not absent from heaven, either.

My dear workers, if you don't " put in time," it *pulls you out.* From what ? And into what ?

From wise thoughtfulness, into silly carelessness. From growing power, into growing weakness. From happiness, into unrest and discontent. From wealth and prosperity, into a slowly eating loss.

Watch your account in the great ledger of life. It is the littles that make the mickle there, even more truly than elsewhere. Heap up a comfortable balance in the bank of character, and you can put into your account there nothing more valuable than bits of time well spent.

It is very interesting to watch the running of express trains on one of our great railways. Every energy is put forth and every device adopted that will bring the train to its destination at the advertised hour. In order that the engineer's attention may not be diverted from his important task by constant looking at his watch, and that possible errors arising from the imperfection of a single timepiece may be avoided, the engineer on some roads is not obliged to look at his watch at all, but, as he flies past the frequent stations, men are seen standing by the side of the track holding up a large dial with plain figures and a movable hand. On one side the dial simply reads, "On time." On the other side the face and hands show how many minutes the train is late. If the "On time" face is presented to the approaching engine, the man at the throttle is happy ; but if the other side confronts him, he must crowd on more steam.

How very convenient it would be if we were favored with such an arrangement at the stations of our life ! If we could only know

whether we are " on time " for all opportunities ; " on time " for God's designs ; " on time "
for fortune ; " on time " for the well-being of
our friends ; " on time " for the higher interests of the kingdom of God ! And if we
are not " on time," if we could only know just
how far behind time we are, and how much
steam we must crowd on to keep up with the
schedule !

But God has not established any such arrangement. I think I know why. I think it is
because he wants us to crowd on all steam all
the time ! I think it is because we are not
" on time " at any point along the line of His
purposes unless we get there just as speedily
as we can !

CHAPTER XXIX.

THE BULLDOG GRIP.

PROBABLY "The Hoosier School-master" is not read so often nowadays as formerly, which is a pity, for it is a sturdy and a delightful book; and therefore it is likely that few workers of the present have the inspiration that I have gained from that bulldog scene. It was a simple enough scene—merely the picture of a bulldog getting that grip upon a raccoon which never lets go until the 'coon is dead; but it made a profound impression upon the Hoosier schoolmaster as he watched it, the spirit of the bulldog got into him, he set his teeth, he conquered the refractory school, and he won his way through other perils that were worse, and all because of the bulldog's jaws.

You remember the familiar lines of sage Dr. Holmes:

"Be firm! One constant element of luck
Is genuine, solid, old Teutonic pluck,
Stick to your aim! The mongrel's hold will slip,
But only crowbars loose the bulldog's grip.
Small though he looks, the jaw that never yields
Drags down the bellowing monarch of the fields."

137

Those resolute jaws under that·tree in Indiana shook out many a tough problem for me in my college days, mastered many a lesson. When my brains begun in every convolution to shrink from the task, when the air of the room settled down upon me like a hot, suffocating weight, when the words in the textbook, from an incomprehensible meaning, ceased to have any meaning at all,—then I remembered Edward Eggleston; I said to myself, " Fool! To be worsted by half a hundred lines of type!" I clinched my hands and my teeth, rushed forward and grappled with that text-book doggedly, got a mental grip upon it that no interruption, no wandering thought, no shout from the campus, no butterfly at the window, could for an instant relax, and I worried it, and I shook it up and down, and got a bigger mouthful, and at last I saw it at my feet—conquered.

It is this element of fierceness that wins battles. There is a certain note which, if a general can ever get into his soldier's yell, means victory every time. Ordinarily we use only the surface of our will, just as in ordinary exercise, so the doctors say, we use only the surface of our muscles. There are exercises, hard and long continued, which bring into play the deepest muscular fibres, and really make a man strong. Something like that is what I am urging for your work, no surface energy, no nibbling with long teeth, but a fierce, savage plunge at the vitals of the task.

It is this that makes the difference between successful farming and fruitless farming—this, among other things: the lazy farmer will not plow deep. As in the old days, yes, and as still in many of the slothful tropical lands, it is held sufficient to scratch the ground with a pointed stick of wood. As Douglas Jerrold said of Australia, "One has only to tickle the ground with a hoe, and it laughs in a harvest." But such tickling of most fields brings a rain of tears rather than a harvest of fortunes. Push through the root mold, thrust aside the disputing stones, press down into the rich heart of things, plow deep, if you would reap a goodly fortune.

All analogies point to this strenuous injunction, and I have little doubt that most workers will promptly accept it as a true guide for successful labor; but recognition of a truth is very different from following it; so very different! The allurements are many, and the flesh is weak. Many a lesson has been a failure because the scholar cheated himself into thinking that what his brain needed was a little rest, that after a game of ball or a

night's sleep the problem would solve itself
before his delighted, invigorated mind. Many
a victory has been lost for the lack of just one
more charge. Many a house has been ruined
because the roof was not clapped on as soon
as the walls were up. Many a crop has been
spoiled because, after it was brought into
heaps, the heaps were not immediately carried
to the barn. It is the long pulls that make
the oarsman, and it is the long pulls that make
the workman. I have a great respect for the
tradesman's sign, " Done While you Wait."
At that shop, at least, there is no dilly-
dallying.

A jolly party of us once spent two weeks
together in the Maine woods, and one of the
jolliest of all was a certain distinguished
clergyman whom we will call Dr. Peace.
Now Dr. Peace, being enterprising, took it
into his head that he would learn to paddle a
canoe—an art he had never yet attempted.
We used to stand on the shore,—all eight of
us,—and double ourselves up with laughter at
his antics. He would be paddling along, a
most determined expression upon his face, becoming a beatific expression as the tricksy
craft actually seemed under his control at last,
and going straight where he wanted it to go.
But, alas! along would come a whiff of wind

and would slue him round in a jiffy. With a mortified and disappointed air he would look up to see if any one was watching, would perceive the spectators on the shore, and try to paddle out of sight, always bringing up in a circle again.

But one day Dr. Peace came into camp radiant. "I've got it!" he exclaimed. "Did you see me? I'm boss at last. No adventitious canoe can get ahead of me!"

"Well, how do you do it?" we inquired with respectful interest.

"How? I back her into the wind. Yes, sir, whenever the wind swings her around, I just back up. So I get where I want to go. Stern foremost? Yes, sir. What's the difference? I get there, sir. I arrive."

This manœuvre of the genial doctor's produced no end of amusement, as we saw it proudly illustrated on the very next opportunity. His progress was a combination of progression, oscillation, and retrogression, but, as he said, he got there. It was not long after this surprising discovery that he became in very truth master of the canoe, and could direct it bow-foremost in the face of any wind.

So much for determination. So much for good-natured grit. We all, I think, took the little lesson to our own lives, and decided that hereafter, though contrary winds might blow around the uncertain craft of our fortunes, we would not lose our course, we would "back her up into the wind," we would not be too dignified to go stern foremost, and in some way—if not in the best way, then in the second-best way—we would arrive.

An artist once showed me a fine bit of landscape—a wind-blown marsh, with a pool in the centre which reflected the blue sky and the dark shadow of a coming thunderstorm. "I spent about ten minutes on that," he said to me; "I had never painted so fast in my life. The light-effects were changing every instant."

"And when will you finish it?" I asked, in my stupidity.

"Finish it? It is done! When the scene changed I could not add another stroke without spoiling it. My chance had been given me, and I had used it."

Toilers, enter upon every task with the ardor of that impressionist painter. You see before you some ideal of achievement. You have the opportunity to transfer it to the canvas of reality and permanence, to make it the world's eternal possession. Grasp the palette with eagerness. Seize a handful of brushes. Eyes intent, hands swift, mind stretched forth like a greyhound in the chase, capture the fleeting vision before the sun goes behind the cloud.

CHAPTER XXX.

ID you ever consider the importance of that gap between the steel rails of a railway? Without it, the expansion of the steel in summer, having no longitudinal outlet, would bend and twist the rail sideways, and our American record of railway accidents would be far worse even than it is. Alas! many a life-train has been wrecked because there were no gaps in the plans along which it ran.

"Make a programme for the day," say the moralists, and they say well; only, they often forget to add, "Insert in your programme a few intermissions." "I will do this," we say in the morning, "and after I have done this I will take up that, and after that I will accomplish the other, and after the other the next thing," and so on through all the hours. We plan to do too much.

One of the results is disappointment, for we cannot do all we plan to do. We end the day with an uneasy sense of tasks still untouched,

144

a docket far from cleared. Others might deem us to have accomplished a good day's work, but the things we meant to do and didn't, blind us to the things we did do. Then come the blues.

We ought to plan for rest, for doing nothing, —or as near to nothing as this work-crazed world can come to. We ought to imitate God's wisdom in nature, and provide seasons of fallow ground and of hibernating. But we expect to go right on raising crops of energy and enthusiasm and all sorts of activity from the same ground, without a particle of the recuperation and fertilization of fruitful repose.

Some folks will think this advice very unwise. They will have in mind the shirks, the sluggards, whom we have to be continually prodding to get them to do any work at all. "They will take your words as an excuse for laziness," urge the critics. Well, let them, then, though they have no business to. If not that excuse, they would have some other. I am not going to permit my care for them to keep me from giving a greatly needed warning to the precious lives that are doing the world's work.

To you, then, toilers, and to you alone, I would cry : " Live for the eternities! There's a year to come after this, and a year after that

year. God does not want you to do it all at
once. God wants you to work as He works,
without hurry or worry, and with a plenty of
joyous repose. Keep fresh—for His sake!
Keep young and vigorous and smooth-browed
—for His sake! Live for His eternity, into
which He wants to welcome us strong and
alert and buoyant, ready for age-long service
with Him."

Now vacations help, but vacations come to
most men only once a year, and go as rapidly
as they are slow in coming. The great vacation, after all, is made up of fifty-two days, the
Sabbaths of the twelvemonth. Those are the
worker's chief breathing-spells, and I should
send out a very incomplete book upon work if
I said in it nothing about Sabbath-keeping.
All ten of the commandments are *working*
rules, but the fourth is preëminently the commandment for workers.

If you want to know whether you are keeping Sunday, ask yourselves earnestly whether
you are *keeping* it. What do I mean? To
explain.

We never talk about "keeping" Monday,
Tuesday, Wednesday. These days have their
fixed and peculiar duties and observances much
as Sunday has, but the truth is that instead of
" keeping " Monday and the rest of the week-

days, they "keep" a great deal of us. They keep so much of us that on Monday night we are usually, if we are common, average folk, a little worse off, physically and mentally,—yes, even spiritually, often,—than we were Monday morning. And so with the rest of the days, up to Saturday night.

I am not saying that it is best, of right, that the week-days should keep so much of our strength and our mental faculties and our good temper and our hope and faith. I am only talking about facts.

But we all have known days at whose end we felt ourselves born into a new life. Since the dawn we have come into wondrous accessions of strength and knowledge and beauty and joy. The day has built itself into a permanent addition to our lives. We have "kept" it.

Such days—whether the first day of the week, or the third, it matters not—are Sabbaths. And such days will all our Sabbaths be, if we "keep" them aright.

This, then, is the test of your keeping of the Sabbath. At the close of the Lord's Day are you refreshed in bodily powers? You have kept it. Is your mind stored with a new treasure of noble thought? You have kept it. Are you happier, braver, more contented, trust-

ful, and loving? You have kept it. But if
you are weary and fretful, sad and selfish, you
have not kept it; it has kept you.

The Sabbath is for the eternities. It is for
permanence. It is for building, for accretion,
for *keeping.* " Is not Monday also for these
things?" you ask. "Have we kept Monday
unless at its close we are stronger, wiser, happier, than at its beginning?" Assuredly, no.
If we look well to our Sunday-keeping, however, we need not greatly fear. We shall then
keep Monday, and Tuesday, and all the days
of the week.

I have just said that our fifty-two Sabbaths
are the chief breathing-spells of the year. That
was a thoughtless remark, for it left out of
account our daily Sabbaths, the holy night-
times. A worker, after all, is made or un-
made, not by his working but by his sleeping
hours.

The well-known Philadelphia physician, Dr.
William Pepper, although he died at the age
of fifty-five, is said to have done as much work
as an ordinary man living to reach one hundred years. This he accomplished through
his enviable power of sleeping just when he
wished.

He would often interrupt a consultation
with a patient by saying, " Excuse me, madam,

but I could talk with you more satisfactorily if I had a few minutes' nap." Throwing himself on a lounge and telling a servant to wake him up in ten minutes, he would drop off at once into profound slumber, from which he would spring refreshed when awaked, and would take up the business just where he had left it.

As he was being driven from one appointment to another of his busy life, he would sleep in his carriage. He could sleep on trains. He would sleep in the parlors of strangers, no matter what was thought of him. In fine, he was a master of somnolence.

That is an art especially to be cultivated in these hurrying, bustling days, these days of nervous prostration and paralysis. We need not become Dickens's Fat Boys; Dr. Pepper certainly did not. But the first requirement of our physical being, proper sleep, is far nearer to godliness than even the cleanliness of the proverb.

Dr. Hale once wrote it as his opinion that a healthy man should be able to fall asleep at any time he chose, and anywhere. A healthy baby can. If this is true, how far from health is the average man! Insomnia, one of the most terrible of diseases, is sadly common. Millions of men and women have almost lost the blessed knowledge of sound sleep. Their nights are as full of tossings as their days of fretfulness and fume. It is the rattle and roar of the iron horse by day, followed, of course, by the nightmare. And to the young —alas and alas!—the fearful contagion of unrest is rapidly passing.

And what is the remedy? Not in drugs, where hundreds of thousands are seeking it. In those drugs lie coiled the chains of one of the most fearful slaveries groaning man has ever known. Not in philosophy or mind-cures, reason how you will. In none of these things; but in this: "I will both lay me down in peace and sleep, for Thou, Lord, alone makest me dwell in safety." That is it. "He giveth unto His beloved sleep."

It is the Christian contentment, the Christian self-denial, the Christian resignation of this world, the Christian peace of conscience, and the Christian joy; it is this happy frame of mind that alone can cure insomnia. In the matter of sleep, as in other matters, the Christian has become as a little child. And we know of no better test of one's Christianity than this.

CHAPTER XXXI.

THE TRIVIAL ROUND.

LADY once heard a friend quote the well-known line from a beautiful hymn, "The trivial round, the common task." "O don't say that!" she exclaimed, impulsively. "I could not stand it if that were all, if it were only a *round*, if the routine began to-morrow just where it left off to-day, and I had it all to do over again without any progress. It is trivial enough—my life,—but it must be more than a circle, or I cannot endure it."

That is the feeling of us all. We can do the common task, we can support the dull routine, if we know that we are getting somewhere, if we see the goal approaching, however slowly. But a treadmill, especially a treadmill yoked to no achieving machine,— nothing in the universe is more dreary than that.

Fortunately, though there *is* a trivial round, and though far too many lives have adopted it as their order, there *need* be no such thing in any life. The rest of the stanza gives the true doctrine. Read:

> "The trivial round, the common task,
> Will furnish all we ought to ask :
> Room to deny ourselves, a road
> To lead us daily nearer God."

So it seems that the " trivial round " which the poet had in view is not a circle or a dead level, but round and round on an ascending spiral, a great winding staircase, hard enough to climb, as we all know, but conducting us through all the damp stones and the darkness and the weariness and the monotony, up to a bright, sunny platform whence the kingdoms of all happiness will be outspread before our delighted vision, for we shall have mounted into the paradise of God.

Our Latest Publications.

Lincoln at Work. By William O. Stoddard.

Finely illustrated by Sears Gallagher. 173 pages, cloth, embellished cover design. Price, $1.00.

Probably no one is better acquainted with the every-day life of Abraham Lincoln than William O. Stoddard, one of his secretaries at the White House during the greater part of the war. In a series of fascinating and most graphic chapters, Colonel Stoddard pictures the gaunt, ungainly young politician, his rapid and marvellous rise to power, and that strange life in the White House, so appealing in its pathos, its quaint humor, and the profound tragedy that lay underneath it all. The author makes us feel as if we ourselves had been permitted to sit by the side of the great President in his dark workroom, or to be present at his momentous and striking conferences with his generals. Many anecdotes are told, throwing a flood of light upon the times and the man, and the whole closes with a powerful picture of the impression produced by Mr. Lincoln's death, even in the South, where Colonel Stoddard was at the time. Mr. Stoddard is an accomplished story-writer as well as a skilful historian, and both qualities come into play in making this delightful and important book.

From Life to Life. By Rev. J. Wilbur Chapman, D. D.

200 pages, cloth. Price, $1.00.

A collection of anecdotes, stories, incidents, poems, and other illustrative material drawn from many sources and touching many topics. A leading feature of the book is the large number of incidents taken from life and carrying their own lessons. The compiler, well known as one of the foremost evangelists, gathered the matter for his own use from his own observation; and the choicest parts have been selected for this volume. It will therefore be of great interest and value to Christian workers generally, whether for their own help or as an aid in winning others.

Doings in Derryville. By Lewis V. Price.

212 pages, cloth, 60 cents; paper, 25 cents.

This story is of a noble young girl who finds herself in one of those many country towns which have quite lost their Christianity and become almost pagan. The church was closed, Sunday was a lost day, worldliness and Satan had full control.

In a series of wide-awake and stirring chapters, Mr. Price describes the organization of a Christian Endeavor society. A Sunday school soon follows, and later comes a pastor, who is willing to use his powers in meeting the great need, and for love of his country and God do what he can to build up the neglected country town. The incidents woven into the story are all actual facts which have come under the author's own observation. Two beautiful love stories sweeten the tale and add to its human interest.

UNITED SOCIETY OF CHRISTIAN ENDEAVOR,
Boston and Chicago.

The Deeper Life Series.

A series of daintily bound books upon spiritual themes by the leading religious writers of the age. Bound in uniform cloth binding. 6 3-4 by 4 1-2 inches in size. Price, 35 cents each.

The Inner Life. By Bishop John H. Vincent, D. D.

"A study in Christian experience" which shows how the life of the soul is the true reality, and what striking results are wrought when the power of Christ and the indwelling of the Holy Spirit become the controlling forces in a life.

The Loom of Life. By Rev. F. N. Peloubet, D. D.

" The threads our hands in blindness spin,
Our self-determined plan weaves in."

"The Loom of Life," and "If Christ were a Guest in our Home," which is also included in this volume, are two very helpful sketches by the author of that well-known publication, Peloubet's "Select Notes." Many new and forceful truths are presented, such as will give the reader thought for serious consideration for many a day. The book abounds in apt illustrations and anecdotes, in the use of which Dr. Peloubet is so skilful.

The Improvement of Perfection.
By Rev. William E. Barton, D. D.

This is not a treatise on the higher life, but is meant to help young Christians to a higher life by showing what kind of perfection God expects, and how it is to be gained, at the same time furnishing an incentive to attain it. The aim is practical rather than theoretical, and the style is clear and attractive.

I Promise. By Rev. F. B. Meyer.

The book is appropriately called "I promise." Its chapters deal with matters of the utmost importance to every Christian, such themes as "Salvation and Trust," "Winning God's Attention," and "What Would Jesus Do?" In strong, sensible, winsome words the path of duty is pointed out, and conscience is spurred to follow it.

UNITED SOCIETY OF CHRISTIAN ENDEAVOR,
Boston and Chicago.

The "How" Series.

By AMOS R. WELLS.

7 1-4 by 4 1-2 inches in size. Uniformly bound in cloth with illuminated cover design. About 150 pages each. Price, 75 cents each.

How To Work.

This is a working nation, and yet few among its millions of workers know how to work to the best advantage and with the best results. The fundamental principles of wise labor are set forth in these chapters in a familiar, conversational style. Much of the book consists of actual talks given to young men and women starting out in life. "Puttering," "Putting Off," "Hurry Up!" "Taking Hints." "A Pride in Your Work," "'Can' Conquers." "The Bulldog Grip." "The Trivial Round," —these are specimen titles of the thirty-one chapters. The book is not didactic, but presents truth in illustrations, so that it *sticks*.

How To Play.

The author of this book evidently believes in recreation. The very first chapter is entitled, "The Duty of Playing." Separate chapters are devoted to the principal indoor amusements, conversation and reading being the author's preferences, and also to the leading outdoor sports, especially the bicycle and lawn tennis. There are many practical chapters on such themes as how to keep games fresh, inventing games, what true recreation is, and how to use it to the best advantage. "Flabby Playing," "Playing by Proxy," "Fun that Fits," "Overdoing It,"— these are some of the chapter titles. In one section of the book scores of indoor games are described, concisely, but with sufficient fulness.

How To Study.

These chapters, on a very practical theme, deal with the most practical aspects of it,—such topics as concentration of mind, night study, cramming, memory-training, care of the body, note-taking, and examinations. The author makes full use of his experience as a teacher in the public schools and as a college professor, and the book is largely made up of talks actually given to his students, and found useful in their work. The chapters are enlivened by many illustrations and anecdotes, and the whole is put into very attractive covers.

UNITED SOCIETY OF CHRISTIAN ENDEAVOR,
Boston and Chicago.

www.ingramcontent.com/pod-product-compliance
Lightning Source LLC
Chambersburg PA
CBHW020949030426
42339CB00004B/9